Venetian Gardens

Venetian Gardens

MONTY DON & DERRY MOORE

Contents

Introduction

To go to Venice in search of gardens might seem to be founded more in hope than expectation. No city is more beautiful or more romantic, but few would stake its claim to fame on horticulture. There are some public gardens but space is so short and so hard won that gardens might seem an impossible luxury for most. But spend any time at all beyond the obligatory visit to St Mark's Square and you will catch glimpses of plants in passing and snatches of possible gardens through gateways and doors. There is wisteria reflected in the water as it falls in swags over a wall, a magnolia hedged between two buildings, or ivy capping a wall in green billows. The signs are elusive and enigmatic, with little clue as to the scale or content of any gardens within – but it is evidence that they are there.

Gardens are essentially rooted in earth and Venice is nothing if not a city of water. However, the two do combine and at times gloriously so. There are few better ways to start a day than stepping from one's hotel straight into a boat and setting off down the back canals and opening out onto the Grand Canal early on a spring morning to visit gardens. No journey in any city in the world is more beautiful and the gardens are all integrally bound into this beauty rather than being exceptional.

Some of this is to do with the way that Venice's existence depends upon the same contract with nature that every gardener deals with. It is a bargain whereby mankind manipulates and controls the natural world to make something beautiful and useful, but on licence – and that licence can be withdrawn by weather, negligence or misjudgement at any moment.

Every church, *campanile*, *palazzo* and *fondamenta* has had to be stolen from the waters and built on millions of wooden piles driven into the mud of the lagoon. Venice itself is actually made up of scores of islands, most of them tiny and interlaced with canals and bridges, as well as the thirty-odd inhabited larger islands in the lagoon. Despite the longevity of its medieval buildings and the incredible labour and engineering skill necessary to make them, there is the constant threat of the sea reclaiming its own. The city is slowly sinking and the waters slowly rising. It does not bode well. Every now and then an exceptional *acqua alta* sweeps away any the sense of a firm footing. Despite having lasted with glory for over a thousand years it is a fragile, anxious relationship. This, of course, adds to the romanticism and gothic drama of Venice, worn by time and tide, dressed in fading finery as it slowly succumbs to the sea.

OPPOSITE – *In winter Venice is stripped back but often wrapped in mist and fog, as here on looking out from the Dogana early on a November morning.*

NEXT PAGE – *Looking east down the Grand Canal towards Santa Maria della Salute and the Dogana.*

Historically gardens originated, as did the *campi*, from open fields and pieces of land where vegetables could be raised. As the campi were paved over the gardens remained, and other than on the Giudecca and the outlying islands – which had the space for larger gardens that could grow a range of vegetables and fruit, as well as small vineyards – they were confined increasingly to small pieces of private pleasure grounds for the wealthy. By the eighteenth and nineteenth centuries gardens were frequently enlarged by buying up and then pulling down adjacent buildings. This trend was radically reversed in the twentieth century when formerly large gardens and parks eaten up by new developments such as the railway station and Piazzale Roma and houses for those working on the projects.

Just as the artificiality and tenuous existence of the city is suited to garden making, so too is the introverted, rather secretive nature of Venetians throughout the ages. In every sense of the word no city state is more insular or inward-looking. Their gardens are hidden and very private partly due to the crowded, condensed nature of the buildings but not least because that suits the Venetian cast of mind.

Whilst there is an inherent secrecy and tribal loyalty to all things Venetian – city over and above country, church and any other Italian region – Venice is also a place of carnival and opera and this is also reflected in their gardens. The idea of a garden as a place where one can enjoy gardening is rarely the primary consideration. They are made as a show, a theatre often designed to be looked down on as though from a box in the opera house. The performance comes partly from the planting and the statues but they are really the setting for people, inhabiting the garden like a stage, who make it come alive. But for all the outward show, it is a private play, probably in Venetian dialect, intended only for the select, trusted few.

Gardens always tell you as much about the people that made and care for them as their plants, and the mysterious nature of Venetian gardens tells us much about Venice. However often you visit – and I have been coming to Venice for over 40 years and Derry over 60 – its beauty never wanes, never fails to intoxicate. It is freshly life-enhancing every single time. But that is only ever part of Venice's story. The sweeping, magisterial views of the Grand Canal, St Mark's Square or across the basin to San Giorgio Maggiore are counterbalanced by the sense that there is always something round the corner, unseen, unknown and perhaps unknowable. However often you visit, it remains the most elusive of cities.

OPPOSITE – *Although gardens are often hidden, window boxes and potted plants on balconies are to be seen everywhere right across the city.*

But gardens are a good way to get under the skin of a culture and to understand its people. *Venetian Gardens* explores some of the most public and the most secretive, the tourist-saturated and the fiercely private, in the most beautiful city in the world. From her gardens we have looked at Venice from the inside out and perhaps reach a little closer into her heart.

THIS PAGE – *Moro's statue by Tintoretto's house, leaning a little, perhaps due to the weight of the enormous turban.*

OPPOSITE – *A canal in Cannaregio, pittosporum billowing out over the water.*

OPPOSITE – *A garden high above the water seen from Fondamenta degli Incurabili*
THIS PAGE – *A statue glimpsed from a* calle *in Santa Croce.*

THIS PAGE – *In early May wisteria flowers all over the city. The huge range of brick colours and textures perfectly compliments the mauve of the flowers and the fresh green foliage.*

THIS PAGE – *Peonies and a grove of tamarisk trees in the Baslini garden on Torcello with the campanile of the island's Cathedral in the distance.*

NEXT PAGE – *Giardini Reali in September, with its seemingly simple but brilliantly sophisticated planting of shades of white and green. Wisteria on the metal pergola, hydrangeas, myrtle, pittosporum and the foliage of agapanthus all harmonise superbly.*

In the distance you can glimpse the statue of Fortune on Punta della Dogana.

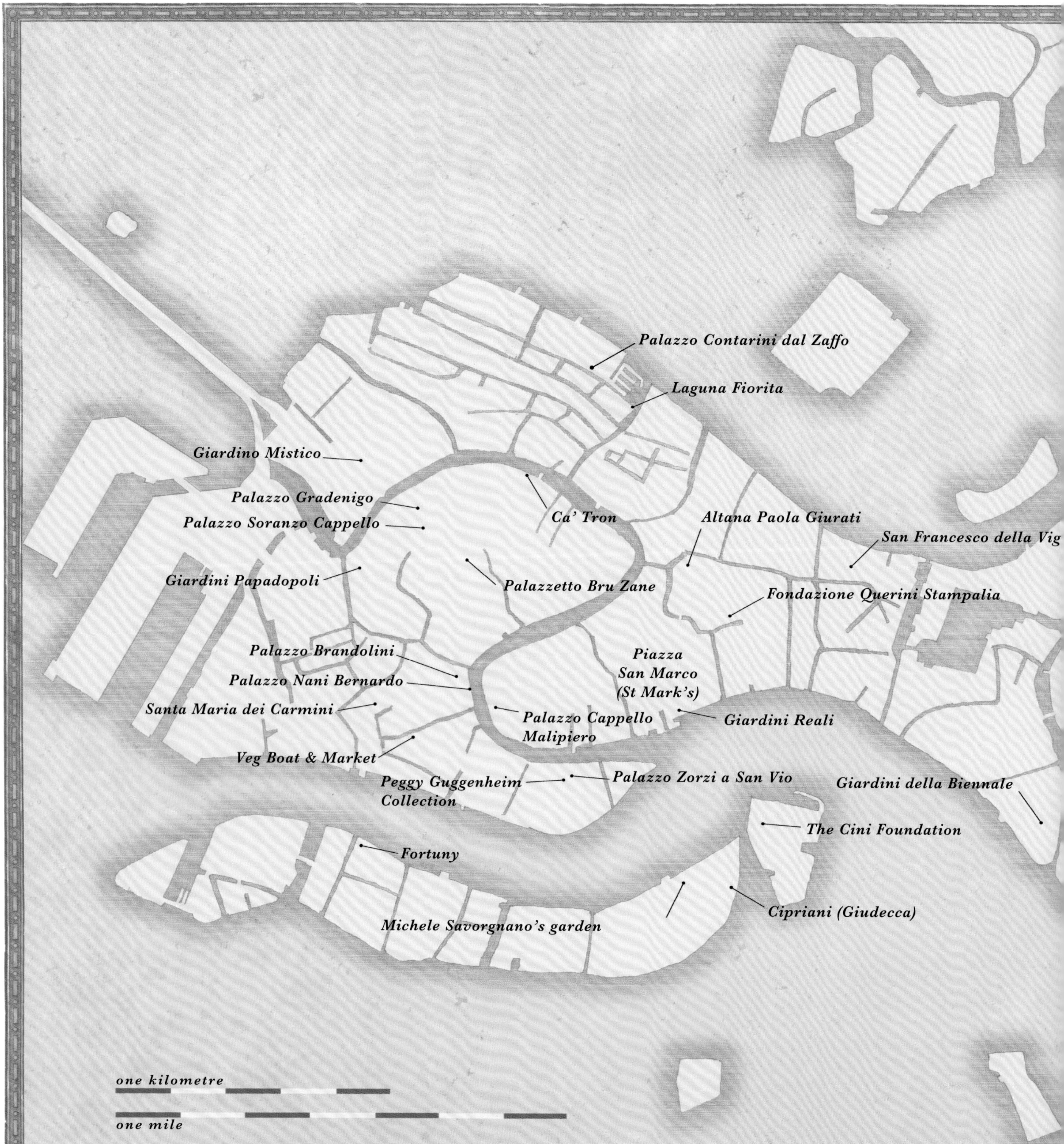

Palazzo Contarini dal Zaffo

Laguna Fiorita

Giardino Mistico

Palazzo Gradenigo

Palazzo Soranzo Cappello

Ca' Tron

Altana Paola Giurati

San Francesco della Vig

Giardini Papadopoli

Palazzetto Bru Zane

Fondazione Querini Stampalia

Palazzo Brandolini

Palazzo Nani Bernardo

Piazza
San Marco
(St Mark's)

Santa Maria dei Carmini

Palazzo Cappello
Malipiero

Giardini Reali

Veg Boat & Market

Peggy Guggenheim
Collection

Palazzo Zorzi a San Vio

Giardini della Biennale

The Cini Foundation

Fortuny

Michele Savorgnano's garden

Cipriani (Giudecca)

one kilometre

one mile

Orto di Sant'Erasmo

Locanda Cipriani

Angelica Baslini

VENICE

Villa Lisa - Pasqualin

Palazzo Brandolini

Palazzo Brandolini, originally built in the seventeenth century with a floor added in the eighteenth, was once the home of Robert Browning, had been a hotel, then a gentleman's club but was then bought by Count Brandolini d'Adda and is now lived in by his widow, Countess Cristiana Brandolini d'Adda. The garden is extremely private and the chance to visit it is a rare opportunity.

We approach by the front door on the Grand Canal, disembarking into an immaculate *portego*, guided by a polite but alarmingly large gentleman to the courtyard garden at the rear. The inevitable stone wellhead is at the centre of the herringboned brick yard, but also barbells, medicine ball and parallel bars with a young man furiously doing sit-ups, guided by a trainer whilst another unusually muscled gentleman watched over them. None of them acknowledge our presence, one because he is seriously distressed and gasping for breath, the trainer because he is concentrating on his job and the minder because he is completely inscrutable. The scaffolding, sheeting and detritus of building work fills one half of the courtyard but despite this and the makeshift gym there is an elegant space evident, backed by the elaborate balustrades and columns – Doric for the first two floors and Ionic for the third – of the building behind.

But up a flight of broad stone steps flanked by statues half hidden with ivy is the 'English' garden. The Englishness seems to derive partly from the loose swirl of greenery that envelops it and partly through the association with Russell Page, the British garden designer who advised on this as well as Cristiana Brandolini's country estate at Vistorta, and although his involvement must have been over 40 years ago (Page died in 1985) the garden has the confidence and simplicity of his hand still clearly on it.

Cristiana Brandolini, a member of the great Agnelli family, is now 95 and permanently accompanied by two charming liver-coloured dachshunds. Despite the initial reluctance to allow us to visit and photograph her garden, she is wonderfully hospitable, funny and engaging. She said that she adored Russell Page – 'so handsome and such good company. He made two lakes at our country place and for two years the men did nothing but dig, dig, dig.'

However, in this Venetian city space the opportunities for dig, dig, digging were clearly rather more limited. It is filled almost completely with a parterre, planted in box, with gravel paths and a gravelled seating area with heavy metal furniture around a low stone table. The parterre is heart-shaped, apparently as a statement of love, albeit time has softened that outline to the point where the heart is hard to make out on the ground and can only really be seen from the *piano nobile* within the building. Box balls are placed in pots hidden within the hedging, rising as finials above it. Like much-clipped box plants across the entire western world, it is all touched with the depredations of blight

THIS PAGE – *Wisteria shades a balcony looking back over the garden.*

THIS PAGE &
OPPOSITE – *As in most
Venetian palazzos, the
courtyard at Palazzo
Brandolini is dominated
by the ornate stone
wellhead. At the far
end steps lead up to
the secluded parterre.*

and box caterpillar and has grown together to the point where the folds and arabesques of the parterre are almost grown together. But it still works and there is nothing that a sharp pair of shears could not put right.

Almost lost in the yew hedge is a memorial stone inscribed with 'AUDREY 2000 – 2014'. I rather hoped it commemorated a dog.

There are no flowers, just green on green, a yew hedge providing a tall backdrop behind which large uncut yews hide the buildings beyond. The only colour comes from the rich terracotta of the flanking building, but it serves the green well and the effect is rich but soothing. The privacy is complete.

Up at the top of the palazzo are not one but two *altane,* although I was shown only the first, the lower, of the two. Cristiana told me that she made it a few years ago when she was unwell and needed cheering up. It opens out from a little sitting room and has a covered dining area crammed with flowers and herbs in pots. Then up a few steps is a roof garden with a diamond marble-tiled floor, a large table and views across the tiled roofs to the mountains in the north and the campaniles of St Marks and San Giorgio Maggiore.

I hope that when I am in my nineties and need cheering I too shall have the energy and relish of life to make a garden.

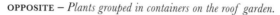

THIS PAGE – *On the ground the parterre is a thicket of tightly woven box hedging, but from the vantage point of the third floor of the palazzo the heart-shaped outline can clearly be seen.*

OPPOSITE – *Plants grouped in containers on the roof garden.*

THIS PAGE – *The roof garden on Palazzo Brandolini was made a few years ago and is both open and completely secluded, free to look out for miles but not overlooked by anyone.*

Palazzo Nani Bernardo

If you are not thrilled by sweeping up in your own private boat to the entrance of a palazzo on the Grand Canal then your life has gone badly astray. Suffice to say, I was thrilled. My life, here in Venice, about to visit a special garden on a glorious late summer's afternoon, was very much on track.

Palazzo Nani Bernardo is next door to the bigger and much more famous – but newer – Ca' Rezzonico. There is no hint of a garden to be seen. But disembark onto the typically simple wooden landing stage and move from the canal entrance into the deep and predictable gloom of the long atrium towards the light glowing green at the end of the dark hall, then on underneath a wisteria-shrouded, covered patio area with a wellhead adorned with ferns and you enter a long, large garden that leaves the wateriness of Venice behind.

Nani Bernardo was built in the mid-sixteenth century on the site of an earlier building; originally its facade faced east, but after the building of the much bigger Ca' Rezzonico on the site of its original garden, Nani Bernardo acquired a new facade facing out onto the canal. Then, at the beginning of the nineteenth century, when the Republic had ended and Venice was flipping between the regimes of France and Austria, a garden, which originally had occupied the site where Ca' Rezzonico stands, was added to the rear of the building. A row of houses were knocked down to clear the ground (their blocked-in doorways with faded house numbers cut into the stone are still a ghostly remnant on the wall of the adjoining calle) and the result was the luxury of space that belies the relative modesty of the palazzo in comparison to its much bigger, more exalted neighbour.

OPPOSITE – *The courtyard of Nani Bernardo is completely roofed with wisteria on a permanent framework.*

THIS PAGE – *The palm tree in front of the parterre lays claim to be the tallest in Venice.*

NEXT PAGE – *A low wall and metal gate divides the shaded courtyard from the parterre. Cannas are in full flower around the palm tree.*

Contessa Elisabetta Czarnocki Lucheschi is the owner and dedicated gardener. Her connection to the place is umbilical. She was born in the palazzo and has lived her whole life there. Her father and grandfather were born there too. Its story is hers, and her life is set irretrievably there and, until very recently at least, the garden had been unchanged for most of the twentieth century.

Bright flares of red cannas are planted in a box-lined bed as you enter. A rumbustious banksia rose fills a corner between house and boundary wall. A palm so tall its fronds rise above the roof, towers above a parterre that fills the centre of this first section of the garden. It is based around two circular rose beds set within concentric box hedges and mown grass defined by more low box hedges. A narrow gravel path bounds it, with long beds down either side of the boundary walls planted with hydrangeas and, slightly unexpectedly, tomatoes scrambling up into the ivy that spills down the wall. 'They were planted by the maid,' I was told in a slightly conspiratorial manner.

THIS PAGE – *Bearded irises line the path and newly planted cypresses replace those blown down in the storm of 12 November 2019.*

ABOVE – *Elisabetta Czarnocki Lucheschi in the garden, attended, as ever, by her dog.*

NEXT PAGE – *Roses fill the borders in the parterre and hydrangeas line the base of the garden wall where a row of houses were cleared in the early nineteenth century to enlarge the garden of Palazzo Nani Bernardo.*

The Contessa shows me her garden with unabashed enthusiasm tempered by notes of regret and apology. At first I take this to be the ubiquitous apologetic note that almost every gardener adopts when showing their garden. The excuses are invariable in tone if not detail. 'Ah, if only you had been here last week/month/year, next month, when the roses are out or the lawns cut'. All gardeners do it, myself included, helplessly apologising for not being able to fix those fleeting moments of personal perfection to suit public display. But in fact the Contessa has real reasons to explain shortcomings in the garden and, for her at least, real loss and regret.

The acqua alta has always been a feature of Venetian life, occurring when exceptionally high tides combine with storm surges whose winds – either the cold bora from the north east or the warm sirocco from the south east – drive water from the Adriatic into the lagoon. This results in flooding that lasts until the tides change, and although causing problems, it is generally manageable or at least a long-standing problem. But over the past century, to support the huge industrial developments at the edge of the lagoon as well as the development of the port of Venice at Marghera, water has been pumped from the aquifers under the lagoon. These act as cushions that support the land mass beneath the water and the result of the extraction has been that the aquifer cushions have deflated and Venice has sunk. At the same time, as a result of climate change, sea levels have risen and extreme weather in the form of exceptionally heavy rain has become more common.

The combination of these factors has made the effects of these storm surges worse and, occasionally, catastrophic. The last such exceptional aqua alta came on the evening of 12 November 2019. This was the worst flood since the notorious one of 1966, with the water rising over 1.87 metres (6 feet). The Grand Canal rose until it poured into the ground floor of Palazzo Nani Bernardo and flooded the entire garden. On top of that, 70-mile-an-hour winds ripped out trees and when the tide fell it left behind the garden saturated with salt water, which resulted in the death of many plants.

Tears filled the Contessa's eyes as she told me this, two years on. I realised that it was not the result of the storm damage that was making her apologetic about the state of the garden so much as sharing a deep, personal loss. The wound was still fresh. She pointed out the three young cypresses planted along the edge of the garden, replacing the three she lost and which she had lived with her entire life up to that night. She had also added olives and a pomegranate, 'For good luck'. I tentatively suggest that these calamities always bring some opportunities – such as more light into the garden. I only needed to look at her face to see that this was a poor trade-off.

However, she pointed out the palm tree that had survived – 'the tallest in Venice,' she said with real pride.

Halfway down the garden is a bed filled with salvias and pink and white gaura, an unexpected prettiness amongst the Victorian stolidity of gravel paths, box hedges and thorny roses. The Contessa's face visibly brightened and softened with affection as we

reached them. She loved them, she said, did I think they looked good like this? Yes, I said – although I thought that any flowers that gave her such clear and obvious pleasure would look and be good.

Beyond this point the garden went on almost as far again with large trees, obviously surviving the storm, a summer house used now as a storage shed and an area left to run free that had once been for vegetables – and which she told me they intended to tackle soon. Perhaps. There was a sense that it was out of sight and therefore largely out of mind and its trees offered screening and shade that was as sustaining as vegetables.

We leave with the Contessa waving us off from the doorway just inches above the water of the Grand Canal, the garden again hidden, folded back into the private life of the household.

THIS PAGE – *The wellhead in the courtyard now flows with ivy and ferns rather than water.*

NEXT PAGE – *Looking through the underside of the large banksia rose whose flowers face out onto the garden.*

Palazzo Cappello Malipiero

Most of the palazzos on the Grand Canal rise directly out of the water with no more than a landing stage to moor up against. Very few have gardens visible from the water, but as our barge took us daily up and down the Grand Canal one garden shone out, a cut above any other, by virtue of having swags of white and pink roses spilling and billowing down to the water over a stone balustrade. In a city of water, stone and brick this was a touch of softness that trees or shrubs could not emulate. With each pass, the desire to go and see the rest of the garden tantalisingly glimpsed between the balusters as we sped by became more urgent.

The garden belongs to Palazzo Cappello Malipiero and is private. Too private, it seemed, to be visited or photographed, let alone filmed by the film crew I had with me. Every day we passed it and every day it looked lovelier. So we asked nicely, pulled strings, asked again, but all to no avail. Then, the day before we were due to leave, word came that we could visit for half an hour that afternoon. So plans were hastily rearranged and at the allotted time we duly presented ourselves at the side entrance on Salizzada Malipiero.

The palazzo was first built in the eleventh century for the Soranzo family but it was largely restored and enlarged at the beginning of the seventeenth century by another of the long-standing patriarchal families, the Malipieros. At the end of the nineteenth century it was bought by the Barnabo family and Contessa Anna Barnabo is the current owner.

Malipiero has a claim to fame which, in a Venetian context, makes it exceptional and fascinating. Giacomo Casanova, libertine, lothario and byword for male sexual conquests, was born in 1725 in Calle Malipiero, a few yards from Palazzo Malipiero, baptised at San Samuele opposite the street entrance and was a frequent and welcome visitor to the household. He was taken up by Alvise Malipiero, a septuagenarian senator, libertine and man of the world, and he became something of a patron to him. Around 1740 Casanova moved into the palazzo, acquiring social skills and graces from his mentor. Casanova seems to have been precocious in all things – entering university in Padua at 12, graduating with a degree in law at 17, as well as beginning his lifelong obsession with dalliance in his early teens. This proved to be his undoing because he unwisely turned his attentions to a young singer who was also the object of Alvise Malipiero's attentions, and when he discovered Casanova in flagrante with the actress Malipiero expelled them both from the house, never, so far as we know, to return – although the incident did nothing to dim Casanova's subsequent enthusiasm for amorous adventures.

The garden has two axes – from the typical Venetian gloom of the entrance hall towards a brightly lit figure of Neptune framed in a doorway. You cross a small shady

OPPOSITE – *Twin statues of Hercules and Antaeus flank the entrance to the garden of Palazzo Malipiero, with the statue of young Hercules wrestling a snake and a Nymphaeum dominated by a statue of Neptune.*

NEXT PAGE – *Looking past one of the statues of the four seasons with the palazzo on the opposite side of the Grand Canal beyond.*

courtyard filled with plants, past statues of Anteus being lifted off the earth that nourishes his strength by an adult, brutish Hercules and out into a gravel path with four rose beds around a central statue, this time of the infant Herculean thug grappling with a rather phallic serpent fountain. Beyond that, at the eastern edge of the garden is Neptune in an elaborate Nymphaeum – half elaborate alcove, half loggia. This was apparently salvaged from Palazzo Cavazza that was pulled down to make the railway station and relocated here.

In each of the four box-edged rose beds around the central fountain are four statues of the seasons by the Paduan sculptor Giovanni Bonazza. So in this relatively small space there are eight large scultpures, a substantial building, a fountain and four largeish rose beds, not to say trees, climbers and lots of pots. The effect is as rich as an ornately decorated eighteenth-century salon and a lesson in how to make a small garden seem much bigger. But then, swivelling at 90 degrees, the second axis runs down to the nineteenth-century balustrade onto the canal.

The garden as we see it was created at the end of the eighteenth century and a print dated 1703 shows the palazzo looking exactly as it does today but with buildings where the present part of the garden fronting onto the canal is. These were duly knocked down, in standard Venetian fashion, demolishing houses, an inn and a vegetable garden to create the space that you can now see from the canal.

In the centre of this view is the large Istrian stone wellhead that was moved from the inner courtyard and is now draped with the procumbent rose 'Snow Carpet'.

A central gravel path runs between a parterre made from more large rose beds and enclosed little lawns, opens out into a sitting area around a stone table, screened from the canal by the balustrade that we passed so tantalisingly. It is like sitting in a box at the opera while the performance flows endlessly, entrancingly, by.

The hedges are kept trimmed and the roses are clearly much loved but in the same way that roses are loved the world over, doing what roses effortlessly do best. But the setting transforms any ordinariness into sublimity. Nowhere else in the world could a small garden, albeit one with eight large statues and water features, be surrounded on four sides by buildings and yet have such a beautiful view.

The palazzo itself and its neighbouring buildings form a tight frame of ochre walls but it is the fourth wall, the view across the canal to the palazzos on the other side, that transforms it. The width of the canal creates room enough to give them balance and remove any sense of being overlooked and overwhelmed whilst retaining proportion and intimacy. It is the most perfect urban setting that any garden might have on this earth.

THIS PAGE – *From the edge of the garden there is the best view in Venice of the Grand Canal.*

NEXT PAGE – *View of the Palazzo Malipiero seen from the Grand Canal, roses tumbling over the balustrade.*

Santa Maria dei Carmini

The barge makes its stately progress off the Grand Canal into Rio delle Muneghette and pulls up by the Campo dei Carmini, which opens up before the curtailed circles of the brick facade of Santa Maria dei Carmini. Over its shoulder, the *campanile* rises, a statue of the Virgin balanced on the very top as a kind of spiritual lightning rod. In fact, the original Madonna del Carmine did her work too well and was duly destroyed by lightning. What we see now is a replacement put there in 1982.

I had been told that at the base of the campanile is a small communal garden created from a piece of lost ground. Finding its entrance involved skirting round the church and dog-legging the narrow calle to the back of the building. Then I had to go through an improbable door that in turn led to a winding passage, which then opened into a concreted, awkwardly angled space. I had reached an *orto* filled with raised beds, people quietly working and – palpably, and from the first entrance – a sense of benign calm.

This odd corner – bounded by the Carmelite monastic buildings on two sides with their enormous campanile, with a wall behind onto Rio de San Barnaba on the third side, and at the fourth, a verandah containing an outdoor kitchen, a coffee machine, shelves of books of all kinds, and a long table for communal meals – was created from

THIS PAGE – *The team at Orto del Campanile is made up of volunteers.*

a rubbish dump. It had been filled with rubble, desks, fridges, soil, stone – all of which had to be removed and taken away by boat. Once the space had been cleared, they built a series of raised beds, now occupied by tomatoes, fennel, rosemary, sage, marigolds, melon, peppers, endive and rosemary. Oranges grow in pots and a vine scales the base of the campanile. In a far corner, a large peach tree is heavy with white peaches.

THIS PAGE – *The campanile of the church of Santa Maria dei Carmini.*

NEXT PAGE – *The raised beds of the garden are filled with soil that has to be brought in by boat. They are made extra high so that they stay above the highest aqua alta – and they also incorporate a seat at the end of each one.*

Per nostra sorella madre te

Netting was stretched tight around the base of the campanile because, slightly alarmingly, 'bits occasionally fall off'. The netting seemed unlikely to do much to save a falling madonna but no one seemed unduly concerned. The fallen all land safely here.

On the side of one of the beds is written in large, looping calligraphic letters '*Per nostra sorella madre terra*'. I confess I had to look it up but it comes from Francis of Assisi's 'Canticle of the Sun':

Laudato si, mi Signore, per sora nostra matre Terra,

la quale ne sustenta et governa,

et produce diversi fructi con coloriti fiori et herba.

(Be praised, my Lord, through our sister Mother Earth,

who sustains and governs us,

and who produces various fruits with coloured flowers and herbs.)

In the shadow of the monastic buildings – albeit of a Carmelite rather than Franciscan order – it seemed an appropriate epigram to grow by. And of course, there is the echo of the Terra Madre project begun by the Slow Food movement started by Carlo Petrini in Rome in the late 1980s. Italy may not have a gardening culture as the British know or understand it, but connect food that has provenance with family and with meaning to horticulture, and you reach deep into an Italian's soul and open the door to gardening.

The raised beds are exceptionally high with 1.2m (4 foot) sides, so that not only are the beds less demanding for backs but also, more pertinently in this city, they are above water when the acqua alta comes to town. In fact, the great flood of November 2019 rose almost to the top even of these beds. 'At least,' I was told with the rhythm of a much-repeated witticism, 'the tomatoes came ready-salted.'

The beds were half-filled with rubble for drainage and then with topsoil that is changed every two to three years. This, like everything else, is brought in, bag by bag, on boats. The point of this, other than the laboriousness of it, is that even the most basic, humdrum elements that make up a garden are expensive.

But clearly it is money well spent.

The people here are all women and it seems that although not deliberately, exclusively so, the place has been largely created by and is run and used by women. The orto lacks the gung-ho competitiveness of so many male-dominated allotments. No one is measuring their veg or weighing their fruit. In fact, no one is being told what they can do. None of the raised beds have been allotted to anyone or belong to any particular individual – I was told that anyone can come in, anyone can plant anything anywhere, and anyone can harvest and take anything as long as they make a contribution according to their means.

THIS PAGE – *The garden is bounded by a canal, the church of Santa Maria dei Carmini – and apartments with, as everywhere in Venice, washing hanging out to dry.*

This egalitarian and incredibly harmonious set-up was instigated and is largely run by an extremely practical, unidealistic Parisienne, Christine Huriet, married to a Venetian. Although loving her adopted city, she longed for a garden, was excited by the idea of gardening as part of a communal enterprise and, with an un-Venetian practicality, made it happen.

Christine told me what I was to hear repeated numerous times, namely that there is little real understanding of horticulture in Italy other than the private growing of some vegetables and fruit for the table. 'Gardening' is regarded as something done by professionals – very few people see it as a recreational or creative activity. However, Christine believes that this is slowly changing, particularly amongst a younger generation, despite there being little opportunity for them to garden. This is much of the appeal of this hidden plot, which is, at the moment at least, a rarity in Venice. There is an official allotment in Venice but only people over 65 are eligible. The young are not encouraged or really provided for and anyway, Christine said, the older generation are very jealous of their knowledge and not very good at sharing it. But the Orto del Campanile is based upon everyone sharing knowledge, time, seeds, produce and companionship. It is most definitely not, like every allotment around the world, somewhere for individuals to have access to their own individual space, but is, in every sense of the word, communal.

Above all, in this city where gardens are either secret and costively private, or are places to meet rather than to engage in any horticultural activity, the Orto del Campanile seems alive and vibrant and yet completely harmonious. 'There is a lot of peace here,' Christine said, as though commenting on a variety of plant or the quality of the light, as though peace were a palpable presence. She is right. In this crammed, claustrophobic, spooky, beautiful city, this modest little orto, created from a rubbish dump in a forgotten corner, is a deep pool of peace.

THIS PAGE – *A wide assortment of pots and containers sits under the shade of a vine trained over a trellis at the base of the campanile.*

Ca' Tron

And so to the Faculty of Territory Planning. Not the most inviting of destinations until you learn that it is housed, as part of the IUAV University of Venice, in Ca' Tron, a sixteenth- century palazzo in Santa Croce, on the Grand Canal, with a garden. The front may face onto the canal but the back is approached by a maze of fondamente, calle, bridges and overhung alleyways. It feels as though one is sneaking in through a secret entrance but once inside the building all is space and proportion. We are shown round, up to the second floor *piano nobile* that stretches the depth of the building, one huge window filled with the green of the garden and at the other end of the room the reflected water of the canal and across to the casino on the opposite side.

The Tron family were one of the oldest Venetian families and had always lived in this parish, and lived here in successive generations from its completion in the 1580s until they died out in the nineteenth century. The Trons produced one Doge, Nicolò Tron, between 1471 and 1473, whose fame mainly resides in growing a bushy beard on the death of his favourite son at the battle of Negropont and refusing to shave it, as an emblem of mourning. The palazzo housed the first public opera house in the world in 1637, starting as a private theatre but soon charging people that flocked to see the operas that were rapidly becoming Venice's most popular art form.

Another Nicolò Tron was Venetian ambassador in London in the early eighteenth century and, inspired by what he saw in the rapidly industrialising northern towns in England, set up the first mechanised woollen mills in Italy, initially in Venice and then in Schio - which in the 19th century became the largest woollen mills in Europe. A reminder that Venetian money, however patrician, artistic or religious the buildings it financed, was always built firmly on trade.

Their garden fitted a standard pattern with the courtyard, the grey flagstones immediately behind the building patterned with white istrian stone diamonds made from quarter circle curves, with an elaborate stone wellhead in its centre. Students lean against this with proper iconoclasm, adding energy and life where respect would quickly lead to neglect. A mauve lilac tree in full flower lends shade to a group of girls sitting on the low wall beneath it.

OPPOSITE – *The courtyard at the back of Ca' Tron features an ornate pattern in Istrian stone centred around the wellhead.*

NEXT PAGE – *From within the piano nobile that runs, as with all Venetian palazzos, the full depth of the building, the light is filtered through the leaves of the trees in the garden.*

To one side, in the area that, conforming to the Venetian pattern, that was probably used for growing vegetables, is a small garden, fenced off, called Giardino Francesco Cannone, after a young graduate from the university who died in 2010. A billow of *trachelospermum jasminoides* in heavy and fragrant white flower hangs in swooping swags from the walls.

Beyond the courtyard is an area of garden raised up by a low step flanked by urns, which once would have been formal but is now dominated by mature trees that shade out much beneath them. There are no less than eight large palms and a superb oak tree shading out the grass, so that by the end of April it is already worn and bare, deprived of light and water and subjected to heavy student footfall.

At the very back of the garden is a high stone wall, on inspection rather grand with a much-worn statue, its protuberances greened with moss, in a recess at its centre. This was obviously the focal point of the formal garden, now lost entirely in the trees. To one side a washing line hangs from the neighbouring building, socks, shirts and sheets dangling tight against the foliage of the trees. Although neglected – there is no sign nor semblance of gardening or care – it is obviously used, and the large trees and lack of horticultural pretension of any sort make it a surprisingly pleasant, rather sexily shady place for students to meet or simply sit and read. This means that, although very simple and barely tended, the garden feels alive and loved in the way that a more mannered and conceptual garden left to be 'natural' could never be.

THIS PAGE – Trachelospermum jasminoides *in heavy and fragrant white flower hangs in swooping swags from the walls within the garden.*

NEXT PAGE – *At the far end of the garden of Ca' Tron a lichen-stained statue stands half hidden in the undergrowth, a ghost of the garden in its formal heyday.*

Giardini Reali

On a hot late-summer afternoon the Giardini Reali, screened from the stream of trudging tourists and the salt winds by green netting attached to the high iron railings, is a deliciously cool, calm respite right at the centre of Venice's tourist frenzy.

The planting, dominated by shades of cream and green, is restrained in colour at this time of year and yet fulsome and generous in volume. This makes the limited space – just over one acre – seem much bigger. This takes great confidence and shows a real sureness of touch.

Plants spill and flow out of the large borders onto the immaculate white gravel paths and yet hold their shape, leaning on each other with easy and restrained familiarity rather than the slightly lurching, toppling growth of many a late-summer border.

A metal pergola clothed mainly with wisteria runs the length of the garden, lined with scores of benches settled within its green shade. The large pom pom heads of *hydrangea* 'Annabelle', the white petals made lime green as the sun filters through the wisteria foliage, billow along its length as a repeated floral refrain. There is not an inch of bare soil to be seen. Liriope and the shrubby butcher's broom *ruscus racemosa* thrive in the shade and outside the pergola, in full sun, the strap leaves of agapanthus, the flower heads and stems all cut off, form a green, grassy under layer to myrtle bushes. Despite the simple colour palette at this time of year that is so easy on the eye, the irises and agapanthus as well as the autumnal colour of the trees must be rich and jewel-like in their season.

Above all, for all its harmony, the planting is an unlikely and surprising mixture where contrasting textures and shapes work as strongly as colour. So evergreen iris foliage underlies the huge splayed leaves of *tetrapanax* which in early May carry mauve and inky blue flowers alongside the rose 'General Schablikine' with its pink, muddle-petalled flowers. Around *hydrangea paniculata* and *Osmanthus* lap the fat round leaves of *Farfugium japonicum*, unexpected but completely satisfying.

Along the back of the garden, flanking the narrow canal spanned by the drawbridge, are large pots planted with pomegranates, citrus, figs and *ziziphus*, the jujubes tree. The whole garden is shaded by trees, such as holm oaks, Camphors and the Caucasian walnut *Pterocarya fraxinifolia*, chosen to be deliberately fast-growing and tall to create another layer of shade. Around the edges of the garden are billowing cloud-pruned laurels, pittosporum and eleagnus, forming an evergreen buffer from the basin, magnifying the prevailing sense of a calm retreat.

OPPOSITE – *The campanile of St. Mark's rises above the rear of the Giardini Reali.*

NEXT PAGE – *An ornate iron pergola, clothed mainly with wisteria, runs the length of the garden, lined with scores of benches settled within its green shade.*

The site next to the Piazzetta San Marco, was for centuries a wharf with fourteenth-century granaries, clearly visible on Barbari's map of 1500 as four imposing facades fronting a broad fondamenta linked by a bridge to the Piazzetta.

Following the disposal of Venice to the Austrians in autumn 1797 and then its return to France in 1805, after the Austrian defeat at Austerlitz, Napoleon tried to impose a distinctive French stamp. He did not visit Venice until 1807 and then only stayed a week, but set out characteristically sweeping schemes 'improving' the city. One of these actions was to knock down the granaries and the church of San Geminiano to expand the new palace and create a garden for his stepson, Eugene Beauharnais, whom he had appointed Viceroy of Italy, so it could have an uninterrupted view out over the basin. This new garden fronting directly on the basin was approached from the new building on Piazza San Marco by a drawbridge across the narrow canal.

Eugene's reign came to an inglorious end after the defeat of Napoleon in 1814 and the Venetian Republic was under Austrian rule for the next 50-odd years but the Imperial garden remained, with formal parterres and a little grove of trees at either end of its long rectangular site.

In 1816 a greenhouse was built in the western corner, with two wings leading off from a circular central area, now beautifully restored – although it is slightly alarmingly given the name of 'the Human Garden' – to become a cooly stylish exhibition centre and office of the President of the Venice Gardens Foundation, Adele Re Rebaudengo, who has been the driving force of the restoration.

THIS PAGE – *The cream flower heads of* Hydrangea *'Annabelle' are the only flowers amongst the evergreen buffer of cloud-like pruned shrubs and hedges that screen the garden from passers by and St Mark's basin. The ornate ironwork of the gates and screen were installed by the Austrian Emperor Franz Joseph in 1856.*

NEXT PAGE – *Cloud-pruned is a familiar horticultural term to describe the (originally Japanese) technique of pruning shrubs to billow irregularly like clouds.*

In 1819 an ornate and rather beautiful casino, built of Istrian stone, was added and now links directly to the greenhouse. This pavilion had a chequered history, being opened to the public as a coffee house in 1856, then in the early twentieth century acted as the headquarters of the Bucintoro rowing club, before, in 1962, becoming the terminal for the new airport where you would check in before a launch swept you across the lagoon to your waiting plane.

At first the gardens were completely private for the Imperial family. But in 1856 Emperor Franz Joseph made his only visit to Venice and gave permission for the public to use the path flanking the basin, but only after high iron railings – still robustly in position – were erected to seal off the rest of the garden. However it did mean that the hoi polloi could peer through the railings at the horticultural splendours of their Hapsburg rulers.

After the First World War the gardens were given by the crown to the state and opened entirely to the public, but throughout the twentieth century the garden suffered indifference and neglect. By the end of the Second World War the buildings were in a state of disrepair, the metal pergola collapsed and the drawbridge unusable. In 2014 the Venice Gardens Foundation set about raising the money and resources for a major programme of restoration and after five years and a cost of over 6 million euros, they reopened in December 2019 – just as the world went into lockdown, Venice had fewer tourists over the coming twelve months than it had had for centuries.

Although there has been a garden on the site for over 200 years, it now feels less like a restoration than like a brand new garden. In this city of horticultural bits and pieces it has a coherent and refined confidence like a well-cut suit on a honed young body. In time it will inevitably outgrow its assuredness and how it is maintained and sustained beyond the level of horticultural housekeeping that is the default position of most Italian public gardens will be the measure of it as a living, lasting garden. But, taken as it is, it is a triumph and a celebration.

THIS PAGE — *A wooden drawbridge, recently restored, connects the garden to what was the Royal Palace and leads through the building to St Mark's Square.*

THIS PAGE – *A pomegranate in a large terracotta pot is the focal point of one of the cross sections of the wisteria-covered walk.*

NEXT PAGE – *Piazzetta San Marco looking out across the basin to St Giorgio di Maggiore. The two columns are topped in turn by the Venetian winged lion and San Teodoro with a dragon.*

Piazza San Marco (St Mark's)

The Piazza San Marco, comprising the wedge-shaped piazza, the dog's leg of the piazzetta heading to St Mark's Basin, the Doge's Palace and Sansovino's Logetta and library, are both the largest open spaces and the most famous buildings in Venice.

The Basilica of St Mark's started as the Doge's private chapel that housed the bones of St Mark and became the state church and the symbol of Venice's place on the fault line of East and West. In front of St Mark's facade, overlooked by the four bronze horses plundered from Constantinople, is the campanile, which, apart from a slight blip in the summer of 1902 when it collapsed and took ten years to rebuild, has stood for over a thousand years. At the other end is Napoleon's would-be palace, never fully realised and now the Correr Museum, but with an austere beauty that feels un-Venetian and yet somehow exactly right.

We take this space for granted, but it is an astonishing thing both to have made and to have retained. So much of Venice is cramped and labyrinthine, with calle barely wide enough to squeeze down and canals too narrow for two gondolas to pass, that its open spaces are great bursts of relief. There are a number of campos that are also large, but none begins to match the overwhelming scale and emptiness of St Mark's. It is an outdoor cathedral, an amphitheatre, contained and bound by buildings rather than sea or sky and this has the effect of making it seem even more awe inspiring.

This generosity of space in such a tightly packed and limited city was an expression of power and grandeur but it was also very practical. It is now a monumental public space but for much of its history it was a place closer in spirit to an Arab souk than a grand palatial forecourt, busy with merchants, market stalls and entertainers. There were races, bull chases and tournaments. Whores, pickpockets and pimps patrolled the arcades and between the columns on the Piazzetta executions took place and bodies were strung up from the poles. Ships returning with goods and plunder arrived at the basin and unloaded at the warehouses, where now the Giardini Reali stands. This, was the busy hub around which the Venetian Republic revolved.

The irony now is that it is the bullseye that tourists target in on. Every single visitor has to go to St Mark's to validate their Venetian experience and seemingly every single visitor does and, having done so, many hardly venture anywhere else in the city. At the same time many Venetians, ensconced in the *sestieri* they and their family have lived in for generations, rarely if ever feel the need to go there at all.

However, if you go early in the morning you can have the place almost to yourself so you can watch the sun slowly leak through and above the buildings into its western corner, and its true glory can be properly enjoyed.

The Cini Foundation

Heading across the water to the island of San Giorgio Maggiore, Palladio's great white-marble facade of the church stands as a perfectly symmetrical, harmonious stage set. It was built at what was the peak of Venetian splendour and richness, with Tintoretto, Titian and Veronese as contemporaries, as splendid and dramatic a scene-setter as anything else in the city. Today it remains strikingly beautiful, but it is the backdrop to a million posed scenes of true romance, cultured charm and selfie schmaltz.

From the vaporetto stop in front, the tourists disembark and traipse dutifully into the church, then when that is done, they go straight back out to wait for the boat to take them across the water again. However, my boat is heading for the altogether more modest, monastic range of peachy brick buildings stretched out beside Palladio's operatic masterpiece, because behind them lie the gardens of the Cini Foundation.

Vittorio Cini was a businessman and collector who made a great deal of money in building and developing heavy industry at Marghera. He embraced Fascism in the 1920s and 30s and became an enthusiastic Blackshirt, rising to become Minister of Communications in 1943. But as the Italian war position collapsed, he either saw the error of his ways or a route to save his skin and made a volte face, publicly renouncing Mussolini. In fact, he was taken to Dachau concentration camp by the occupying SS. However, his son Giorgio organised his escape from Dachau in June 1944 by bribing guards, and Cini escaped to Switzerland. It was the subsequent death of Giorgio, aged just 30, in an air crash in 1949 that prompted Vittorio Cini to abandon politics and concentrate on philanthropy. He was granted the island of San Giorgio Maggiore by the state and restored the monastery there, establishing the home of the Cini Foundation intending it as a centre of culture, with a major library as well as a training establishment of the arts and, slightly tangentially, of sailing. It quickly became, and remains, an important curator of Venetian historic and modern culture.

The barge swings into the dark gape at the waterline and judders into the low-slung, vaulted boathouse. A doorway takes you from the cellar-like gloom straight into Palladio's double colonnades around the first cloister, known as the Cloister of the Cypresses – although now notably cypress-free. This was designed in the 1560s as part of the plans for the Benedictine church, but was not begun until the last year of his life, in 1579, then not completed for another 50 years.

But its slow creation does nothing to diminish its glory. The simplicity of its layout and ingredients does not detract from the impression of completeness. Although fully a garden, it is barely gardened. Only two plants feature – grass and box. It is fixed, static, changing imperceptibly across the seasons, and yet dances.

The grass, the day I visited, was shaggy and uncut. Weeds poked through here and there. The box hedging sprouted erratic growth like an unshaven teenager, some circles more recently trimmed than others. It looked not so much neglected as temporarily set aside, as if its owners had returned from a long holiday. By conventional British public gardens standards, a good spruce-up was overdue. There is a sense of hair uncombed, a button undone. But set against the lovely pink stucco walls – part flaking, part repainted – it looked ravishingly beautiful, impossible to improve, let alone perfect, and to worry about any particular horticultural detail, a few weeds here and unclipped section of hedge there, is to miss the point. It's like in an old building worrying about a bit of stone that's chipped or a bit of paint flaking. The show is everything.

THIS PAGE – *Palladio's double colonnades around the first cloister, known as the Cloister of the Cypresses, although now occupied by a box parterre rather than cypresses.* Courtesy Fondazione Giorgio Cini, Venezia.

Walk right round the quadrangle along the cloisters on a bright September morning and see the garden as a gentle strobe of sliced green circles filtered through the ionic pillars, and the show is the fusion of poetry and opera. It is breathtaking.

For the record, the central path is extraordinary. Garden paths tend to be as narrow as possible. For two people you need 1.5 metres, and generosity begins at about 3 metres. But paths take up potential planting space and cost a lot to lay, so keeping them as narrow as possible with the overall scheme tends to be the rule. But this path is fabulously wide. It is a broad, generous swathe. The paving stones are also set longways, so the eye is swept forward ahead and along it. All this adds energy to the enclosed monastic space, where harmony can sometimes become a little prim and airless.

The second courtyard, The Cloister of the Laurels, is part of the oldest section of the monastic complex, begun by Giovanni Buora in 1516 and completed by his son Andrea

THIS PAGE – *The circular box patterns of the first cloister with the church of San Giorgio Maggiore in the background.* Courtesy Fondazione Giorgio Cini, Venezia.

OPPOSITE – *The modern labyrinth dedicated to the Argentinian writer Jorge Luis Borges with the campanile of San Giorgio Maggiore rising behind it.* Courtesy Fondazione Giorgio Cini, Venezia.

by 1540. The laurels have long gone, and it is dominated by four huge cypresses set on the corners of crossing paths and meeting at a wellhead in the centre of the courtyard. The wellhead is decorated with a bas relief of Saint Lucia di Syracusa, patron saint of light and sight, whose remains were preserved in the monastery until the thirteenth century, when they were moved to the church of San Lucia near what is now the railway station in Cannaregio. (In fact, the original church was destroyed to accommodate the station and rebuilt in 1861 as San Geremia, with Lucia's remains inside, they had been shipped and dispersed widely since her death in 304 AD, making her way to Venice as part of the loot from the thirteenth-century sack of Constantinople.)

The four squares made by the paths are lawns. The result is not really a garden but a green carpet flooring the space between the colonnades. For all its greenness it becomes a courtyard. Why is the first cloister a garden true and this one not so? It's hard to say, but it is to do with the relation to buildings, space and the manipulation of plants that defies formulation. Not that it is worse or better than an official garden. Just different.

Carry on through the narrow corridor at the far end and you come to the latest, very gardened and much-feted labyrinth, added in 2011. It was designed by Randoll Coate, an English diplomat and long-standing labyrinthian, to honour his friend, the great Argentinian writer Jorge Luis Borges. Apparently the entire thing came to Randoll Coate in a dream and, like all mazes, it is indulgent, complicated fun and magnificent in its ambition and scope. It is made from 3,000 box plants and symbolises Borges' love of Venice, the city's labyrinthine streets and, when viewed from above, spells out the writer's name. Unlike the cloisters it is meticulously cut and cared for, but starting to show serious signs of box moth depredation, especially at its far end. I fear that box mazes, along with clipped box hedges, will all too soon become impossible to protect, however heavy they are with conceptual gravitas.

The Benedictine monastery existed from 982 until 1806, when Napoleon dissolved it. For the next hundred years or so it became a military barracks and weapons depot and gradually fell into disrepair and decline. However, in 1951, it was granted by the government to the Cini Foundation, who still run it as a cultural centre.

Today the monastery has an anomalous atmosphere. The Palladian church and courtyard have the ecclesiastic grace and harmony bedded deep in Venetian history, whereas the island at large, with its gymnasiums, outdoor theatre, sailing school and art installations have a slightly Eastern-European feel of an unhealthily wholesome summer school. It is an uneasy mix.

THIS PAGE – *The second courtyard, the Cloister of the Laurels, is part of the oldest section of the monastic complex, begun by Giovanni Buora in 1516. The laurels have long gone and it is now dominated by four huge cypresses.*

Courtesy Fondazione Giorgio Cini, Venezia.

THIS PAGE —
Doorway. Courtesy
Fondazione Giorgio
Cini, Venezia.

OPPOSITE — *Avenue
of plane trees in
the garden at the
rear of the monastic
buildings.* Courtesy
Fondazione Giorgio
Cini, Venezia.

The Cipriani (Giudecca) & Locanda Cipriani (Torcello)

To reach the Hotel Cipriani on the Giudecca, you are collected by the hotel's launch, a kind of leather and highly polished wood shuttle service, but much more like a 1950's Bentley than any airport bus. We are accompanied by a group of highly groomed young women, expensively but casually power-dressed, each of whom opens their laptops the moment the boat sets out. It turns out that these are the attendants of the super rich who are taking over the entire hotel for a three-day wedding. It is that sort of place, a byword for luxury, glamour and, speaking from personal experience, superb and friendly service.

In a city where any kind of swimming pool is an exceptional luxury, the Cipriani boasts the biggest. The story behind its exceptional size, true or false, is a good one. Apparently when the pool was built in 1968, the Guinness family, which originally

owned the hotel from its inception in 1958 until 1976, drew up plans for it, putting the dimensions in feet and inches. However the Italian builders, unfamiliar with imperial measurements, converted these to metric, thereby making the finished pool three times the size intended. Whether the story is true or not, the pool with palm trees reflected in its Olympian expanse of blue water, surrounded by ranks of immaculate white loungers and the perfect planters filled with white daisies and immaculately clipped box balls all creates a suitably expansive Hollywood glamour. Although deserted at seven o clock in the morning, clearly this is the outdoor hub of the hotel.

On the other side of the building there is a garden with lawns, a vine walk underplanted with roses and a pergola whose wisteria flowers are astonishingly noisy with the buzzing attention of bees. Herbs are laid out in squares, one for each herb, sage, parsley, oregano, mint and thyme make an aromatic chequer board, all of which are used daily in the kitchens. There is a small vineyard, the walls and dome of Palladio's Chiesa di Santa Maria della Presentazione rising high behind it, whose grapes do not reach visitors' glasses. In fact, although looking entirely ornamental, they are harvested by a farmer on the mainland and made into his house wine.

THIS PAGE – *The swimming pool at the Cipriani is in itself a Venetian rarity but is also Olympian in its dimensions. However, early on a spring morning it is completely empty.*

Fortuny

On 14 July 1902 the campanile in Piazza San Marco collapsed in on itself like a detonated cooling tower. No one was hurt, other than the caretaker's cat, and remarkably little collateral damage was caused other than the end of Sansovino's Logetta being torn off. It was both a catastrophe and one of the most exciting things that had happened in the whole history of the city. Photographs taken in the ensuing few days show a cone of powdered rubble in front of the Basilica, with figures posing on its slopes like Edwardian mountaineers.

Ten years later, on 25 April, the Feast of St Mark, a thousand years to the day that the foundations were first laid, it was officially reopened having been rebuilt exactly as and where it was. What could be seen as a symbol of Venice's decay and collapse of power was turned into a triumph of confidence and durability.

THIS PAGE – *The Fortuny showroom's wonderfully stylish letter box.*

THIS PAGE — *White Japanese wisteria,* Wisteria floribunda Alba, *and the Chinese* Wisteria sinensis *growing together in the Fortuny factory garden.*

Amongst other celebrations that April, a grand ball was held in Piazza San Marco. The presiding genius of this was Marchesa Luisa Casati. She lived at Palazzo Venier dei Leoni on the Grand Canal, which was later to become the Guggenheim Museum. Photographs show her as a red-haired, wide-mouthed beauty with an intense and dangerous gaze in her huge dark eyes. Artists vied to paint her portrait and the novelist Gabriele d'Annunzio was one of her lovers. Her clothes were never less than spectacular, often outlandishly so as she constructed every appearance as a self-proclaimed work of art. She was, as well as being the most celebrated muse of her day, Master of Staghounds in Rome and clearly a fully paid-up character.

Her arrival at the ball of 25 April was preceded by a water-borne orchestra, trumpeters, three falconers bearing their birds upon gloved wrists and the pair of cheetahs that always accompanied her as she walked through the city naked save for a decorously enveloping fur coat. And the costume she wore, on this the most public and dramatic of all stages, was a dress making her look like a Greek deity, made from yards of silk designed and made by Mariano Fortuny.

Fortuny is no longer a household name save in the most rarified and fashion-conscious households, but by 1912 Fortuny was not just the most celebrated designer in Venice but becoming so across Europe.

I confess I had never heard of Mariano Fortuny until 1980, when Sarah and I went to an exhibition of Fortuny dresses at the Museo Fortuny in Campo San Benedetto. I recall the display consisted of silk dresses on a number of mannequins, all full length and elegant with characteristically pleated folds. This was, I learned the famous Delphos gown, essentially the same as worn by Luisa Casati and deeply fashionable for those that could afford it in the first few decades of the twentieth century and which had become iconic in the 1970s. Sarah, amongst millions of others, coveted them. However, as the last one was made in the early 1950s they were rare vintage pieces and cost

THIS PAGE – *The private quarters of the owners opens into a tiny but exquisite courtyard.*

NEXT PAGE – *The courtyard between the factory and the house has its walls smothered in* trachelospermum *and a beautifully pruned* pittosporum *casts dappled shade onto the stone slabs of the yard.*

upwards of two thousand pounds each back then, so this was as close as we or most people were likely to get to one.

I learned from that visit that Fortuny's dresses were always considered a cut above mere fashion. They were art. They were wearable poetry. Their secret, over and above the mysterious business of 'cut', was in the fabric itself, all designed and made by Fortuny and his workshops. These originated at the fifteenth-century Palazzo Pesaro, which came to be known as Palazzo Fortuny in 1956, seven years after Fortuny's death when it was given to the city as a centre of culture, with two floors made over to workshops and studios. An insight into Venetian life is that when Fortuny first came to the building in 1898 and took one large attic room as a studio it was minutely subdivided with over 300 tenants occupying it. Gradually Fortuny bought them out until by 1907 he had the entire building as his workshop and home.

Mariano Fortuny always thought of himself as a painter rather than what we would now call a fashion designer. He was born in Spain but he and his family settled in Venice when he was 19 after a period of studying in France and Germany. Although he continued to paint all his life, it seems he was always extremely practical and fascinated by technical processes and constantly experimented using light, fabrics and dyes as well as techniques of heating fabric to give it texture, such as the famous pleats first of his silk Knossos scarves and then the Delphos gowns. He patented a number of these techniques – most notably the secret pleating process of the silk.

But as his business grew he needed more space to create his unique fabrics and in 1919 Fortuny bought a convent on the waterfront of the Giudecca, facing the Zattere, and built a factory there, designed exactly to his specifications and explicitly to produce his fabrics. It opened in 1922 and from the outset no visitors were allowed inside. This was to preserve Fortuny's trade secrets and, I suspect, to preserve his mystique. In any event it obviously works and works well because it is still going, still secret, and is the last surviving factory in Venice.

The significance of this is doubly stressed by its next-door neighbour, the Molino Stucky, which was built as a vast castellated flour mill and pasta factory at the same time as Fortuny started to occupy Palazzo Pesaro. It was and still is by far the largest building in Venice, but its decline began after the First World War and it finally closed in the 1950s and sat empty for almost 50 years, a huge monolithic symbol of Venetian industrial decline and fall, before being redeveloped as an equally vast castellated hotel belonging to one of the large American chains. It's now a symbol of Venice's only real surviving industry – tourism.

Despite its neighbour's travails, the Fortuny factory has continued, unchanged, unaffected, employing about 30 people, to produce exclusive cotton fabrics with their Renaissance – and Islamic – influenced designs and idiosyncratic textures, that sell around the world. There were grounds attached to the factory, but it seems that Fortuny had no interest in gardens and none were developed in his time.

Elsie McNeill was a New York interior designer who loved the fabrics, came to Venice and became the American distributor, then opened a Fortuny shop in New York in 1928. After Fortuny's death in 1949 she bought the company and took over the running of the whole business and it was she that made the garden. This was as much a business decision as a horticultural one.

Although there is a house on the waterfront looking out to the giant yachts moored on the Zattere, where Fortuny and then Elsie McNeill lived, the garden was not an appendage of this. Other than a tiny but exquisite courtyard linking to the larger and equally lovely factory yard, it was never intended to be domestic. This was horticulture as a business accessory, created expressly to be a place where Fortuny fashion shows could be put on and where buyers and customers could be entertained.

THIS PAGE – *The original box hedges lining the paths were ruined by box caterpillars, so these yew hedges have replaced them and were planted – fully grown – in a day.*

To that end Elsie managed to obtain permission to build a swimming pool – an astonishingly unusual thing in Venice then as now – and the blue water reflecting the clear blue Venetian sky amidst pools of rich green grass shaded by magnolias, oaks cedars and limes immediately sets the slightly sybaritic tone, an unexpected but rather successful hybrid of British Home Counties and Palm Springs. It is a garden perpetually waiting for a party to make it come fully alive. However, it was ironic that by the 1960s, as the garden became established, the Fortuny name was all but forgotten. The exhibition that Sarah and I went to in September 1980 must have been amongst the first flickers of renewed interest.

OPPOSITE & THIS PAGE – *The swimming pool is the centrepiece of a garden specifically designed for parties and entertaining customers and press.*

THIS PAGE – *The stone arch is entirely decorative and leads nowhere but it serves perfectly to frame the wisteria in full flower.*

When I visited in September, a flanking pair of long box hedges had just been grubbed out days before as it was irredeemably afflicted with box moth caterpillars. A team arrived to replace it with yew (*Taxus × media 'Hillii'*) and hundreds were planted in a few hours due to the imminent arrival of the current owners from New York to make an instant, albeit somewhat gappy, hedge. Visiting eight months later the hedge had grown remarkably and looked good. The box hedge may be dead, but long live the yew.

Alongside the factory wall behind one side of this hedge grew a huge Banksia rose, smothered with thousands of small yellow flowers and wisteria, both lilac-coloured and white, hung thickly from metal supports. More roses bloomed pink and red from another, slightly random pergola that led from one open grassy area to another with no particular sense of departure or arrival – unless of course a party was in full swing, in which case the garden became the ideal backdrop, making perfect horticultural sense.

Ironically, the little courtyard between the factory and the house has a real sense of space and place, missing from the 'proper' garden. It is simple, even plain, but beautifully balanced with its central marble wellhead festooned with ivy, the terracotta-coloured brick walls clad in the rich green leaves of trachelospermum wrapped tightly around the shuttered, secret windows, and beautifully shaped and pruned pittosporum cast dappled shade onto the stone slabs of the yard.

Elsie McNeil continued to work at the factory past her 100th birthday but in 1988, by which time she was well into her nineties, she sold the company to her lawyer, Maged Riad. She died in 1994 and the Riad sons, Mickey and Maury, now run the business. It was their imminent visit that prompted the urgent hedge planting.

And what would the Marchesa Luisa Casati have thought of this garden? Would she have entered it to applause, preceded by her cheetahs and her falcons, her Fortuny dress trailing behind her? In fact, just as this most English of gardens was being made in Venice, La divina Marchesa was in London, ending her days in a seedy bedsit. She is buried in Brompton Cemetery along with one of her stuffed Pekineses.

And, to show how small this world can be, her only granddaughter married a cousin of mine, the politician Woodrow Wyatt. I remember meeting her as a small child when she came to our house and that she had, even by the standards of the day, very big hair. Although in the surroundings of our real but very unVenetian 1960's garden, I am pretty certain that she was not wearing a Fortuny dress.

The Giudecca with Michele Savorgnano

You could see that Michele liked the dash he was cutting as he collected Derry and I from the Hotel Cipriani, sweeping his open wooden boat in a loose arc through the ultra sleek Cipriani launches, his long hair, beard and bright orange shirt with broad braces exuding a freedom that the perfectly liveried staff disdained and longed for in equal measure.

We hopped on board and he headed the boat along the back of the Giudecca, past the grand houses, some of which Michele gardens for, that are shielded by walls and hedges from most of the passing gaze.. He points out the Volpi garden, much talked about and which we very much wanted to visit but which remained resolutely closed to our most persuasive entreaties. As well as the homes of the rich and grand there were boat yards with cranes, upturned hulls, a vaporetto hitched high and dry out of the water and boiler-suited mechanics stripping engines. Traditionally the Giudecca was where the boatmen lived, a working community navigating, making and maintaining boats of every kind without whom Venice could not function at all. But that has all but gone and the boatmen live where they can, including the mainland, commuting by car and train to their watery work. We slid by a few fishing boats with nets drying. Michele told us that the only remaining fishermen in Venice now lived in his campo – all the rest were on outlying islands in the lagoon.

The Giudecca has always been apart, only just Venice, almost 'campagna'. This still pertains, with a sense of a having an immediately apparent separate identity. Perhaps this is how Venetians see each of the sestieri, their loyalty and identification to them much stronger and more direct than to the vaguer Venetian whole – although in fact the Giudecca is part of the Dorsoduro.

The Giudecca was the one part of Venice that had a long tradition of quite sizeable gardens and the beautiful and astonishingly detailed maps of the sixteenth and seventeenth centuries show the large gardens of the Giudecca with orchards and vineyards as well as kitchen gardens and parterres. Almost all are gone and built over, but Michele is doing his best to resurrect the notion of a communal garden in his campo.

This is not some kind of organised do-goodery, bringing people together in one horticultural endeavour as much as a healing process. Italy, and in Venice the Giudecca in particular, is very much more at ease with communities that share and bond informally. Michele simply wants people to grow things both in their own available spaces and in shared ones. To this end he provides plants, seeds and expertise as well as boundless energy and enthusiasm.

THIS PAGE – *The campo around Michele's own garden has become, under his guidance, a communal space, where residents freely garden.*

THE GIUDECA WITH MICHELE SAVORGUANO   115

Before visiting his own garden he took us to the Convent of Cosmo and Damien, which has a series of artistic studios and workshops in the old cloisters as well as a large grassed space that he wanted to make a garden in but was rebuffed by the authorities. Michele stores his plants – a medley of hostas, heucheras, geraniums, crocosmia and some very healthy looking acers, mostly rejected from the gardens he works in or rescued from the waste taken to the mainland to dump – so they are ready to distribute to any that want them, as well as for the public borders.

These are apparent as we walk to his house. Fringing the path and under the soft orange brick of the convent are long thin strips of marigolds, kale, artichokes, parsley, mallows, lemon balm, mint and the odd bright petals and spear-like foliage of bearded iris. It is an horticulturally incoherent, joyous jumble, all apparently grown by seed that he provided but was selected and sown by children.

On the grass in front of the apartment buildings, below the washing hanging from pulleyed lines stretched from the balconies, are patches of shanty gardens, gardens rising from the grass as if by experimentation. There are tables with pots filled with bright flowers, vines trained on makeshift scaffolding poles, crates of vegetables and a young woman is busy excavating a planting hole in the grass ready to take the lavender bushes she has by her side.

THIS PAGE – *The gardens arise naturally in an ad hoc fashion, sometimes improvised from pots, furniture and found objects to make something almost instant and other pieces planted with an eye for a longer future.*

THIS PAGE – *Michele has crammed his small garden with plants, mostly edible, and also a little shed made from recycled material, devoted to making that most un-Venetian of items, garden compost.*

THIS PAGE – *Michele gathers the woody prunings of all sizes from the various gardens he maintains in the city and brings it home to cut and neatly stack for firewood.*

THE GIUDECCA WITH MICHELE SAVORGNANO 119

All this has taken place since Michele came to live in this district a few years ago. Out the back of the house that he takes us into is his little garden. This was a completely empty space a few years ago when he bought it but it is now crammed both with plants, including fruit trees, vines, climbers, a wide range of vegetables and herbs as well as a composting area, stacks of immaculately cut firewood (recycled from the prunings of his day job) and above all else, clearly a love – reverence even – for the craft and tools of making things. Everything in the garden, from the sheds, the planters, the terracing and the furniture to the plumbing and electrics has been made by Michele with his own hands using old tools and recycled materials, all of which he uses as part of the garden's adornment as well as its creation. It is a stylish antidote to the slick smartness of wealthy Venice and the Chinese-made tourist masks and fake 'Murano' glass filling an increasing number of the city's shops at the expense of local stores.

THIS PAGE – *Michele Savorgnano.*

OPPOSITE – *Michele has a love of old hand tools and in his garden they are both much used and important decorative features.*

The Peggy Guggenheim Collection

I remember my wife and I visiting Palazzo Venier, which houses the Guggenheim Collection, after a slightly bacchanalian lunch and sitting looking out over the Grand Canal next to Marini's priapic horseman and being the only visitors in the entire gallery for a full 30 minutes. That was when the Peggy Guggenheim Collection had only been open for a few months, a year after her death. Now, more than 40 years on, the queues to get in are constant and it is one of the most visited places in Venice.

THIS PAGE – *The Peggy Guggenheim Collection is housed in Palazzo Venier dei Leoni on the Grand Canal. This looks more modern than it is – it was actually built in the eighteenth century.*

OPPOSITE – *Looking eastwards down the Grand Canal from the roof of the Guggenheim building.*

The tourists come to see the art collection amassed by Peggy Guggenheim during the 30 years that she lived in the Palazzo Venier dei Leoni in the Dorsoduro right on the Grand Canal above the Accademia Bridge. The low-slung, single-storey building is curiously out of kilter with its neighbours fringing the Grand Canal, and for years I assumed it was a 1930's fascistic intrusion, but in fact it was built in the eighteenth century, the low Istrian stone facade convincingly foretelling architectural fashions of the early twentieth century.

There are lots of garden sculptures, particularly in Italy, but the garden of the Guggenheim is explicitly a sculpture garden – the Nasher sculpture garden, to be precise – with works loaned from the Nasher collection based in Dallas, Texas. The role of the garden is to provide a setting for the artwork rather than the artwork enhancing the garden. Nothing is compromised or made less valid by this – gardens come in many shapes and guises – but it is an essential precondition of enjoying and appreciating it as a garden.

Not that most visitors would be looking to do so. They come to see the sculptures and that they are outside is just a variation on the gallery experience. But creating a garden that serves primarily as a backdrop, enhancing the sculpture but not becoming a distraction, let alone stealing their thunder, takes some skill. Confident restraint is called for and has been very successfully applied.

The garden has been skilfully assembled to provide a setting where visitors can move freely and the light can play through the foliage of the trees and clipped box, the ubiquitous pittosporum, acanthus, and ferns creating a green backdrop. Birch, magnolia, whitebeam and cypress trees provide scale and height in the courtyard spaces and enact out that old garden trick of big things making a small space seem bigger.

One of the strange things about much sculpture is that it often looks best in an unlikely or constrained environment. I have long admired the work of David Nash whose burnt, monumental, carved greenwood pieces I find thrilling. But I remember walking the Forest of Dean sculpture trail and coming across a burnt log artwork of his that lost all the strangeness and freshness that characterises his work and looked, set in the woods, like – well, a pile of half-burnt logs. I had seen a very similar piece by him a month or so earlier in a white-walled London gallery and it was riveting. Context is almost everything and sculpture outside often looks best in a garden not blending in and not sitting easily in its surroundings.

So at the Guggenheim the bronze of an Arp or a pencil-thin Giacometti figure are thrilling beneath the shade of a lime in the courtyard and the three Henry Moore cast-bronze figures on a high white stone plinth make the ferns that surround it richer, more fascinating plants. The dissonance creates a setting that is more than the sum of its parts, creating a unique garden from very ordinary planting and arguably enhancing the sculptures.

Another dissonance in the garden is a classical stone rotunda, incongruously capped by ivy like a rich green tea cosy. But Peggy Guggenheim's ashes — along with those of 14 of her dogs — are interred here

Up on the flat roof the view of the Grand Canal, with the Accademia Bridge to the left and the St Mark's basin out to the right, is so breathtaking that the carpet of astroturf is all but forgiven.

THIS PAGE – *The marble Byzantine throne that Peggy Guggenheim bought for the garden when it was still private.*

OPPOSITE *Peggy Guggenheim's ashes – along with those of 14 of her dogs – are interred under this rotunda.*

THIS PAGE *– The garden is designed as a series of enclosed spaces, empty in themselves but which provide the ideal setting for sculpture, either on temporary exhibition or as a permanent home.*

Palazzo Zorzi a San Vio

On the Fondamenta Zorzi on the opposite side of the canal to the Guggenheim Museum and round the corner from the exquisite little rose-filled Campiello Barbaro, wisteria spills over a wall and clambers halfway up a tall cedar. A door leads into the garden of Palazzo Zorzi, now broken into apartments that are lived in by six different families. The garden is split lengthways into two, one section the original kitchen garden, the Brolo, and the other includes the courtyard and formal gardens. Despite the division, both are surprisingly big spaces, expanding out in that particularly Venetian way.

The Brolo runs down the side of the palazzo to make, I was assured, one of the largest private lawns in Venice. It is freshly mown and black planters have been freshly filled with shiny leafed dipladenia, as yet unflowering. But the wisteria along the side of the building is on an heroic scale. I count seven separate plants, all growing vertically, all clearly planted for maximum effect in minimum time – gardening for owners rather than owners gardening. In fact it is owners in the plural – this section is owned by three different families, so quirkiness or individual tastes are unlikely to feature.

But the garden pleases for all that and an ancient Judas tree is allowed to remain, the main trunk lopped off and completely hollow but with three stems growing precariously from it, each candiflossed with tiny magenta flowers emerging directly from the wood.

The other side of the garden is looked after by one owner, the Jarach family, and although sparse in flowers and less obviously tended, it is touched with individual character. A wooden barrier across steps to the main garden keeps seven tortoises away from the courtyard which, as well as the inevitable heavy stone wellhead, has a seating area completely covered with ivy and an untrammeled banksia rose. The trees, like the sea-eaten pallazzos in the streets around them, are old and falling gently apart, propped and patched but still alive. Another ancient and very eaten-out Judas tree – clearly a partner to the one on the other side of the dividing fence – is at 45 degrees and supported by a brick pillar thicker and more substantial than the tree itself. On the other side of the garden a pittosporum also slants over at the same diagonal, kept up by an ivy covered post. A tall yew casts shade that is gloomy in the afternoon spring light but must be delicious in high summer. The grass is worn and flowers few, and yet it is clearly used and loved. It is all very Venetian.

THIS & THE NEXT PAGE – *The Palazzo Zorzi is divided into two separate gardens. On the one side there is the much-used garden of the Jarach family, tended by them, that used to be the main formal garden of the palazzo and is now dominated by large propped and leaning trees and on the other (page 130) the original Brolo or vegetable garden that now chiefly consists of what claims to be one of the largest private lawns in Venice. This part is owned by three different families and maintained for them in the more normal Venetian manner by contractors.*

Giardini della Biennale

Napoleon oversaw the end of the Venetian Republic in 1797 but did not visit it until November 1807 and only spent a week there. However, in that time he made typically sweeping suggestions to change the city. Not least of these was the proposal that this city of small campi and hidden private gardens should have a large public garden or park. The furthest point of Castello was deemed the appropriate site and although heavily populated by lacemakers, fishermen and glass-bead makers, as well as a hospice for retired sailors, a seminary and three large churches, all were cleared away to create this new green playground.

The original plans involved formal vistas and planting, very much in the French style, along with bath houses, a botanical garden, barracks and parade grounds, a cafe and a coach house, all centred around a circular temple on a hillock containing a statue to Napoleon. These plans were quickly scaled down but by 1808 demolition had begun and was completed two years later.

But the French Republican ideal of immaculately maintained gardens as a public source of entertainment and improvement never took hold. Then as now, there was little enthusiasm for maintaining public gardens, and in 1887 nearly two thirds was hived off to become the site of the Esposizione Nazionale Artistica, which in turn became the Biennale, with art and architecture exhibitions alternating yearly. This

THIS PAGE – *Landing steps leading up into the Biennale Gardens.*

THIS PAGE – *Large trees fringe both sides of the Rio dei Giardini.*

NEXT PAGE – *The public park of Giardini Sant'Elena is the largest open space in Venice, where families come to picnic and play beneath the grid of pines.*

means that the major chunk of Napoleon's grand scheme for public gardens is now only accessible with a hefty entrance fee (25 euros at last reckoning).

But the frontage of the Biennale Gardens and the remaining public park across the bridge to the most easterly island of the city, Sant'Elena, is used and does have real charm.

Strolling along the Viale Giardini Pubblici in spring with the basin opening out to the Lido and busts of Wagner and Verdi amongst the gingkoes and hackberry trees, there is a sense of relaxed pleasure, the new foliage dappling a green shade onto the lunchers and skate boarders, the small children running free. At the end of Viale Garibaldi, Napoleon's new road that swept away houses to create a suitably grand approach to the gardens, is the Serra dei Giardini, with its glass-house featuring palms and a fine place to have a reasonably priced lunch – which, in Venice, is a find in itself.

Cross over the Ponte dei Giardini and you come to a simple green park planted with a grid of umbrella pines, holm oaks, a Lime avenue. This is the Parco delle Rimembranze and is in itself it is nothing remarkable but it is the biggest accessible open space in the city, and used by local people in a way that the Biennale park is not – and perhaps closer to Napoleon's original concept, albeit much less formal. This is where you can come and picnic on the grass and people do, sitting beneath the great pines with rugs spread out. It feels unlike any other part of Venice, although between the trunks of the trees, the Lido is just across the water. Children kick a ball around, use the adventure playground and make use of the bike paths whilst dogs mooch around eyeing each other up or chasing balls.

Viale IV Novembre is that rarity, a road like any road in a thousand other parks around the world save for the fact that no car has ever used it. Like the picnickers and children playing in the grass, it is normality but with a Venetian twist. Through the trees are cafes used predominantly by locals, the whole scene as near to Venetian life stripped free from tourism as you will find anywhere in the city.

OPPOSITE – *In the Biennale Gardens the bandstand with its wisteria hat provides a shady place for locals and tourists to eat a sandwich or just rest awhile.*

The Lido

In 40 years of visiting Venice I had contrived never to visit the Lido. It is, of course, detached, but no more or less so than any of the other many islands that make up the lagoon. Yet true Venetians still think of the Lido as 'campagna', along with the rest of Italy. A combination of seeing *Death in Venice* 50 years ago and the endless helicopters hammering across the sky of the lagoon in September ferrying Hollywood stars to the film festival, led me to expect a beachside version of the rest of the city. But, after a busy journey across the lagoon, chopping and bouncing in our little boat amongst the wash of a stream of *vaporetti*, barges and boats carrying lorries, earthmovers and tiers of cars, the reality came as a shock: buses, cars and motorbikes, and roads cluttered with signs and parking bays. The few canals were more like Amsterdam than Venice and the atmosphere is as Californian as Venetian.

Our journey was ostensibly to see a single plant, but a magnificent one. Wisteria in Venice is hardly rare in spring but a particularly fine display was promised and, when we reached Villa Lisa, duly delivered. It was worth the culture shock.

Villa Lisa, owned by Annalisa Rossani, was built in 1912 as part of the great early twentieth-century development of the Lido when it went from being used mainly as a military range and for local bathing to a premium international resort. There are two wisteria adorning the faded yellow stucco of the front, one that was planted immediately after the house was built, whose main stem is now as thick as a tree trunk, and the other in the 1950's by Annalisa's father who had bought the house in 1939 from a Jewish family, the Luzzakas, who fled fascist Italy to go to America.

THIS PAGE & OPPOSITE – *The yellow stucco walls of Villa Lisa on the Lido are the backdrop to an especially fine wisteria.*

CDs dangle amongst the lilac racemes of flowers, their plastic glinting designed to keep away the pigeons that eat the flowers which, as well as creating this overwhelming display, provide the ingredients for the wisteria jam that Annalisa makes every year. A row of aeoniums in pots stud the top of a balustrade and a pair of palms and magnolias flank the front but that really is the extent of the garden, which is tiny compared to the footprint of the house. But everything is an attendant lord that fills a scene or two around the wisteria that is the towering star of the show.

We walked a mile or so further down the Lido, dodging cars and scooters, to a small garden in a backstreets. The outside was not particularly auspicious but within was a bigger, brighter, more scintillating collection of flowers than anywhere else I had seen on the lagoon.

Daniella Falchetta Dona Dalle Rosa was that rare thing in Italy, someone who loved not just gardens and plants but actual gardening. Amongst the collection of fine-leafed maples were scores of tree peonies, all in fulsome, ruffled bloom, bearded irises in rich caramels and purples, white valerian, lilacs, and still some tulips and daffodils. All were grown with great care and skill, hidden away behind the high fences and screening trees in this side street with cars parked outside.

THIS & THE NEXT PAGE – *Some of the tree peonies in the garden of Daniella Falchetta Dona Dalle Rosa.*

Angelica Baslini

We head slowly but steadily north through the shallows of the lagoon, past San Francesco del Deserto with its abandoned brick buildings curiously sturdy and out of scale with the diminishing patches of land they stand on, past Mazzorbo and Burano where, Michele tells us, the houses painted are in candy colours 'so the fishermen, returning in fog, can know which are their own houses' on through the archipelago of swirling islands patterned in the water to Torcello, once the preeminent centre of the lagoon.

Those days are long past and hardly any of its historical glory remains, the buildings dismantled and the stones shipped in a thousand journeys to Venice as material for its succession of palazzos and churches. The shell of the seventh-century cathedral with its campanile remains and astonishing twelfth-century mosaics, now fully restored, attract boatloads of tourists who stay an hour or so, take pictures of themselves and leave. Whereas it once had a population of thousands, now the permanent residents are almost down to single figures and a great deal of imagination is needed to envisage the island's former splendour.

But there are holiday homes and we visited one, Villa Baslini, with an extraordinary garden. It is out of the ordinary not so much for its exceptional horticultural merits, although they are there, but because it is in many ways so unusual. A few hundred yards beyond the grassy ghost of the old piazza, over the unparapeted Devil's Bridge through a narrow track flanked by marshy fields, you arrive at a small gate leading to a wisteria tunnel and a glimpse of mown grass beyond. There is an awful lot of mown grass in the four hectares of the Baslini garden, but fascinating set pieces sit like islands in this tightly shorn lawn lagoon.

Most extraordinary are the semi-excavated ruins of the monastery of San Giovanni e Evanolisi that was built on this site 1,500 years ago. Originally this had been a Roman basilica and then became a monastery for orphans before, like so much of Torcello, being dismantled down to the ground with the stone taken to Venice. The excavated area is enormous, although this reveals only a small part of the site that stretches from the current house to the lagoon with sections of above-ground walls and grassy mounds hinting at what lies below. All of this was excavated by the current owners when they bought the abandoned house and site in the 1960s having come across it when out hunting duck in the marshes of Torcello.

OPPOSITE – *A large pine dominates both ends of the swimming pool that was created from the mound of spoil from the archeological excavations of the monastery of San Giovanni e Evanolisi.*

NEXT PAGE – *The grove of tamarisk trees with their black trunks and thin shoots are very simple but exceptionally beautiful. A piece of gardening genius.*

The garden skirts around the archeology almost as though, head averted, it is pretending not to notice. A long, long pergola carrying a vine runs from a large white stone fountain in front of the house that spills with bedding plants rather than water and leads to more expanses of grass. A vineyard stretches to one side, also neatly mown. A covered paved area, the pillars supporting wonderfully gnarled wisteria trunks forms another island. It is all a little odd, unsettling even, because it is fascinating and the atmosphere is good even though all the conventional horticultural messages are in a strange language.

But there are two truly wonderful things. The first, a swimming pool elevated up on a great mound of soil made from the excavated spoil from the monastery, is inspired. At either end a great pine centres and shades the view and the banks of the mound are sculpted with clipped clouds of bay and pittosporum. Alessio, the gardener at Baslini, told me that there is salt water just 60cm below the surface 'which makes growing most plants very difficult'. If that is so, how much more difficult it must be to create a swimming pool deep enough to be worthy of the name. So the order of things is reversed. The building with all its hints at huge and heavy stone substance is sunk underground and the pool, whose waters are almost invariably down below ground level is set up high on a great earthen tumulus in order that it might have the luxury of depth.

The second thing is alone worth the trip to Torcello. Like so many pieces of garden genius it is startlingly simple: just a grove of tamarisk trees in a grid, their black trunks rising clean from mown grass, their branches pollarded hard so each sprouts a thicket of thin branches carrying feathery, almost effervescent foliage. The trunks, once all straight, now slope and cant this way and that, sending shadows crossing diagonally across the grass. Tamarisk are both very wind resistant and also will tolerate high levels of salt. Their fine, thin foliage means that their demand for water is much less than many trees and they have deep roots that will find what water there is. All in all they are ideally suited to Torcello, with its exposed, salty position and scorching dry summers. Thus the combination of extreme practicality and startling simplicity has made a piece of breathtaking gardening land art.

OPPOSITE – *The campanile of the Torcello Cathedral framed in the garden gate.*

THIS PAGE – *Villa Baslini – and much of Torcello – is surrounded by marshes with the salt water just 60cm below the surface of the garden.*

NEXT PAGE – *View of the lagoon from Sant'Erasmo towards Le Vignole island.*

Orto di Sant'Erasmo

The morning was chilly and a mist hung low on the lagoon. Venice, never an early starter, was not yet awake and only a few delivery boats were out on the water. Cutting through the Arsenale we stopped at Canale di San Pietro to collect another passenger, who swung deftly on board before the boat docked, rucksack slung over one shoulder, a trowel and saw holstered on its cover. This was Michele, our guide for the day who knew the lagoon and its waters intimately and was, he said, the only professional gardener in Venice.

We went past Vignola where a range of crops were grown; Lazzaretto Nuovo, where in the fifteenth century sailors had to quarantine for 40 days before being allowed into the city; a wide canal used by seaplanes in the Second World War; and manmade islands fringed by sandbags to stop erosion, made from the spoil from the construction of the Mose – the flood barrier said to end all future disastrous aqua altas. But we chugged slowly past all of these heading to Sant'Erasmo, the largest island in the lagoon and which for centuries has grown much of Venice's fruit and vegetables. Until 1966 the island grew a great deal of fruit too but the disastrous aqua alta of November of that year destroyed all the fruit trees so the islanders changed to horticulture and now specialise in the long slim purple artichokes of the region. There are fields of them, in rows of finely cut glaucous foliage. It is early May and the season of the tiny buds, or *castraure*, which sell for 1–2 euros each in the floating vegetable stores and are eaten raw, grated on a risotto or pasta. In true Venetian fashion, the artichokes from the lagoon, young or fully mature, are considered by Venetians to be the best in the world.

Michele hands me a glass bead, blue, white and red bands fused by flame. 'This,' he said 'is the price of African gold.' They were made, he told me, by the tens of thousands, sometimes as a product in the glass factories of Murano but often by women at home in a very amateur way, then used to trade in Africa for gold. Many found their way into the rubbish which was, for centuries, gathered up from the city and brought out to Sant'Erasmo as compost to fertilise the soil. Most times that he has visited the island, he told me, he has found a bead or two.

THIS PAGE & OPPOSITE – *Sant'Erasmo is famous for its long, slim purple artichokes that grow by the thousand in its fields.*

THIS PAGE — *There are areas of Sant'Erasmo where the soil is not good for vegetables but very good for vines, as Michel Thoulouze has discovered – he makes fine wine and the magnum bottles are still kept cool, stored in the waters of the lagoon.*

'Look at the rows of artichokes,' he says. 'See how close together they are?' That is because now the fields are fertilised by pellets and there is no need to allow space for barrows to spread the compost. The boats no longer ferry Venetian compost because it is now illegal to spread household waste, so it is taken to the mainland to be dumped and pellets are used. As a result the silty soil structure is degraded and becoming lifeless. There is a small grove of young fig trees, grown as standards, and some potatoes, peas and chicory but all on a small scale. An artichoke monoculture prevails. It is a familiar Italian story. This, the land of the greatest food and produce on Earth, has a terrible environmental record.

But this agricultural, earthy patch of watery Venice, for all its ecological carelessness and neglect, is beautiful. There are areas of Sant'Erasmo where the soil is not good for vegetables but very good for vines, and hard against rows of artichokes a vineyard, *orto Veneziana*, has swaggering hens patrolling the rows and a modern winery, all gleaming steel and tubes, inside an old barn tucked in amongst the trees. The magnums are still stored in the waters of the lagoon to keep them chilled and the wine, even early in a cool spring morning, tastes very good indeed.

THIS PAGE –
*Artichokes for sale from
a vegetable seller in the
Dorsoduro.*

Orto di Sant'Erasmo   155

Altane

Anywhere and everywhere in Venice you see rickety-looking wooden constructions perched on top of the tiled roofs. Some are clearly more substantial and designed but a surprising number look like they have been cobbled together with minimal DIY skills.

Blonde or golden hair with a white skin was an essential component of medieval and Renaissance Venetian idealised beauty. However few Southern Europeans were (or still are) born with naturally blonde hair and fewer still retain it into adulthood. Artifice was needed. To that end there were a number of recipes involving a surprisingly wide range of plants – ivy, sage, rosemary, bear's breeches (acanthus) and fennel all boiled in rainwater is one potion. Fresh ginger and alum mixed with ash and boiled in rainwater is another, and another has egg yolks, honey, saltpetre, barley straw, saffron, cumin and chopped rhubarb amongst its tinctorial brew.

Of course, another complexity to this process was that exposure to midday sun (the sun had to be hot to attain maximum bleaching) would burn and bronze skin that had to be milky white for true beauty. Blond hair and tanned skin was a self-defeating combination. So the Venetian women developed sun hats, broad of brim but without a crown, so their hair could be pulled up and out over the brim, the whole effect like a hirsute umbrella. As further cosmetic enhancement, they used Venetian ceruse, which was a mixture of water, vinegar and lead. The latter being very poisonous and leading, if not to death, to hair loss and skin damage. But then, as now, Venetian women were not alone in being prepared to suffer in the name of beauty.

Altanas were the ideal place in which to expose hair to sun without the indignity of the predatory male gaze. When Mary McCarthy published *Venice Observed* in 1961 she says that altane were 'now chiefly used for hanging out washing'. But 60 years on, many have become highly prized roof gardens.

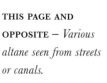

THIS PAGE AND OPPOSITE – *Various altane seen from streets or canals.*

THE NEXT PAGE – *Palazzo Contarini Polignac seen from the Canal Grande with an altana visible in the background.*

The altana of Paola Giurati is in Castello, just off Campo Maria Formosa, just round the corner from the Querini Stampalia. The roof was reached from narrow stairs and featured two separate areas, two roofs, linked by steps. The first was bristled with cacti and succulents of all kinds on racks and shelves around their dining table where, Paola said, they ate on most evenings. She is a Russian teacher, not Venetian born but went to university there and has lived and worked in Venice for the past 22 years, and twenty of them have been in this apartment with these altane. A line of scented pelargoniums above the stairs ward off mosquitos and a passiflora climbs on wires overhead to provide summer shade.

Down a couple of steps to the second area and the atmosphere is very different. The floor is paved and surrounded by high mesh trellising smothered with plants but allowing glimpses of the waves of terracotta roofs beyond. The campanile of the Friary de la Vigna is visible in one direction, that of Saint Mark's in the other. The slightly harsh spikiness of the cacti is replaced with the softness of lavender, a banksia rose, hibiscus and lots of peonies. As well as flowers spilling freely there are strawberries, lettuce, lemons and oranges and an entire range of herbs all growing in containers. Paola has a house and garden in Crete where she goes as often as work allows. When I ask who waters all these pots, exposed as they are to the Venetian summer sun, she laughs. 'Oh that is never a problem. Friends are very happy to water the plants as the rent for staying in an apartment right in the middle of Venice.'

As we leave a present is pushed into my hand, heavy and hard. It is a jar of their home-made marmalade from the oranges growing on the altana. I wait until I am back home, a thousand miles away, before I open and taste it. It is delicious and I am transported back to Venice, in the evening sun, high on the roof tops.

OPPOSITE – *Pelargoniums are planted along the edge of the stairs as it rises to the altana specifically to fend off mosquitos that are distracted by their fragrance.*

THIS PAGE– *Paola Giuriati's altana seen from the street below.*

THIS PAGE – *The higher level of Paola's altana, where they often eat at night, is planted with cacti and succulents.*

Fondazione Querini Stampalia

Carlo Scarpa is the most famous modern architect to come out of Venice. He was born there in 1906, studied there, and his memory is honoured, yet little of his work is openly visible in the city. There is not one complete building of his – most of his work involves interiors such as the Olivetti shop in Piazza San Marco or details, albeit distinctive and meticulous, in other buildings. But fragments and a fluid combination of influences and materials characterise Scarpa's work, so the fact that there is no substantial, emphatic building or buildings as a monument to him is in some ways apt and accurate.

He famously worked very slowly, studying, adding, refining and immersing himself in details of construction and material, rather than coming up with a grand plan that would then go through the laborious process of realisation. This approach suggests to me that the transitory and evolving nature of a garden is perhaps a more apt and more substantial legacy.

Between 1961 and 1963 Scarpa remodelled the ground floor and the garden of Palazzo Querini Stampalia. This is a sixteenth-century palazzo in the Castello district, opposite the church of Santa Maria Formosa. It is a public library and art gallery and was bequeathed to the city by Count Giovanni Querini in 1868 'to promote the study of worthwhile disciplines'.

Scarpa's design is a series of geometric shapes and materials that draw on a mixture of influences. Scarpa was very aware of and had a lifelong fascination with Venice as the meeting place of Western and Eastern cultures. Here, the classical, Gothic and Hapsburg worlds (with a little Art Deco stirred into the mix) merged and re-formed themselves with influences from the Ottoman and Byzantine empires and cultures, not to mention influences that filtered through from further east. Scarpa also had a personal interest in and lifelong absorption with Japanese design and culture (he died in Japan whilst on a visit there in 1978). The garden shows clear borrowings and influences from Japanese tea gardens, with the use of views from inside the building framed by large windows and doors, the meticulous and small-scale use of water, the reliance on and importance of stone, and the limited but heavily symbolic use of plants and planting.

As always, the architectural meeting of the very modern with the very old is curiously satisfying. Sixteenth-century brick and stone sit comfortably next to concrete, plate glass and burnished brass. And the architect's eye constructs the garden as a series of interlocking and interrelated spaces, with some minimal but heavily significant ornamentation.

OPPOSITE – *A small lily pond reflecting the trees in both the water and copper surround.*

You arrive from a light, almost delicate, wooden bridge across the canal into a polished stone-and-brick portego linking water to building, the portego having low walls to hold back the higher tides and deliberately adapted to be submerged during the acqua alta. From there you continue through a large low stone hall, between Doric pillars, into the garden. Like the entrance spaces, the garden is open and minimal, and although small, it feels monumental.

It is completely enclosed by the palazzo on two sides and by an enormously high wall wrapping around the other two. It is as though the garden is the bottom of a tall, ivy-clad, open-topped box. A lawn occupies most of the space, raised up behind a low wall from the entrance path, like the baize of a billiard table, set up above the highest anticipated flood.

But then the detail emerges. Behind the wall is a stone rill with water lilies patterning the surface. Because of its very low water pressure, Venice has never been a city of fountains but Scarpa creates water features on a minimal, bejewelled scale. Two gently trickling pipes feed into a small, labyrinthine sculpture and then the water makes its way, barely moving, back into the rill.

There are hardly any flowers this bright September day. Some honeysuckle and, high on a wall, the orange flowers of eccremocarpus. Small trees – a pomegranate, cherry and persimmon – are clearly carefully positioned and pruned yet, despite this, seem rather random. Clearly the idea and the positioning was particular but the slightly half-hearted pruning, or lack of it, omits any of the Japanese precision that would make sense of them. The Italian love of a design concept has been submerged by the lack of Japanese rigour in maintenance.

Behind the trees is a shuttered concrete wall fronted by a a small square pond, where, clearly, Scarpa was much more at home. The meeting of concrete and Istrian stone and circular swirls of water have a visual confidence and articulacy that are missing from the plants.

Few architects really understand gardens because the thing that makes them good architects stops them being good gardeners. The results are often beautiful and stimulating spaces, with a series of static vistas dominated by hard landscaping, but ultimately they are rather like fascinating stage sets where plays are never enacted.

But none of this is a judgement on the garden. It is much heralded as one of the very few horticultural works left by Scarpa, one of the most respected and honoured modern Venetians. One architectural reference book refers to it as 'a poetic meditation on the dialogue between old and new', which says much about the way that almost all architects approach designing a garden. All plants, even the very oldest, are new. The

THIS PAGE – *Carlo Scarpa used shuttered concrete, Istrian stone, mosaic, metal and water to marry Byzantine, Classical and Japanese influences.*

only meaningful dialogue in a garden is across seasons, not centuries. On the other hand, the garden should not be judged alone but as part of Scarpa's work across the whole building, and the contrast between the old parts of the palazzo and Scarpa's additions are beautiful and stimulating.

Works by great architects tend to inspire reverence. Acolytes pay homage, even go on pilgrimages to great buildings. But solemnity does not serve any garden well. The transience and impermanence of gardens are part of their magic and beauty. They are a play upon life with a fragility and even frivolity that are important keys to the delight they offer/bring. A garden is like flesh and blood, rising to a bloom before wasting and shrivelling. But – and here is your reverence should you need it – unlike flesh and blood, they rise again with the seasons.

THIS PAGE – *Scarpa's steps leading from the garden to the canal gate.*

Window Boxes

There has always been a popular Venetian love of flowers. The word 'florist' was coined by an English visitor, Sir Henry Wotton, in 1623 to describe the flower sellers in Venice hawking their wares grown and gathered on the mainland, and for which they obviously had a ready market. Even when any chance to garden is impossible flowers still adorn most buildings. When I made my first visit in 1980 I remember being struck by the number of window boxes and pots on windowsills and balconies – all of which seemed to contain identical trailing pelargoniums. I had never seen pelargoniums before, having been brought up in 1960s England where they were always raised in hothouses fuelled by great Victorian coke boilers. There, they were only ever used as components in formal bedding. In Venice, the ubiquity of these pink flowers set against trailing olive-green foliage did nothing to lessen their attraction. It was as if the whole city was adorned by one unifying hand and the window boxes became like mouldings, part of the fabric of the buildings.

In fact, all green growth in Venice is almost always seen in the context of buildings whether directly or in the background. The lovely warmth of old brick is perfectly harmonious with the hundred different shades of green. There is no open green space to speak of; except on the edges of the city every tree, climber or shrub is always partly obscured as you pass. Instead, they grow above and through and round the walls that screen gardens or the buildings themselves, almost as though rooted organically in the structure. They spill out over and through the buildings, struggling for light and space, as though the fabric of the city is an ill-fitting lid that cannot contain the greenery which one day will spread and submerge all the buildings before it finally sinks, trees and all, into the lagoon.

OPPOSITE PAGE – *Almost every building has window boxes or plants in pots, and stone, brick and the plants merge to become one organism*

THIS PAGE – *The yellow flowers of sedums are ideal for window boxes because they barely need any watering.*

OPPOSITE – *The courtyard of the apartment where Paola has her altana is filled with the rich green softness of plants.*

174   WINDOW BOXES

THIS PAGE – *The top half of trees, like these in Castello, are a common sight as you pass, hinting at the unseen garden below them.*

THIS PAGE – *Sunlight and shadow in the Dorsoduro.*

OPPOSITE – *Trees making the backdrop for laundry strung out between apartments near the Arsenale.*

THIS PAGE —
*Pittosporum is
ubiquitous in Venice
and these particular
ones billow over
railings like
green clouds.*

Laguna Fiorita

Laguna Fiorita, on Fondamenta dell'Abbazia in Cannaregio is Venice's best known nursery and garden centre. Our barge slides along the Rio de Noale and moors alongside Chiesa dell'Abbazia della Misericordia, just before the canal opens out into the marina on the edge of the northern lagoon. You enter a narrow path and into an open space formerly occupied by a building, with the surviving exterior walls shielding the boats that pass with a steady, uniquely Venetian, motorised hum.

It is less a nursery and more what we would think of as a garden centre, a plant shop, a smallish outdoor display area handsomely stocked with plants, a couple of tunnels and – to my delight and surprise – an enormous pile of garden waste ready for composting. There are also sheds filled with no less than ten mowers plus shredders, rotovators, and to the eyes of this obsessive user and connoisseur of gardening tools of every kind, all well used, noticeably compact, noticeably expensive and desirable. However I learn later that the heap of garden waste is not composted here but collected by a barge and taken to the mainland by a farmer. The concept of recycling or the virtues of homemade compost are much less observed than the virtues of tidying away garden waste so it is out of sight and out of mind.

So, if not a standard nursery, certainly not your average garden centre either and, despite the modesty of its size, much better presented than average. The plants were not just laid out by the standard loose horticultural grouping – annuals, herbaceous perennials, shrubs and so on – but set, in their pots, like borders, tiered on hidden staging rich with suggestions of plant association. Small trees were understoreyed by shrubs and they, in turn, carpeted with plants of various size, shape and colour – but with an emphasis on colour, albeit stylish and tastefully so. Lovely terracotta pots are stacked under a simple cartshed-inspired lean-to, seemingly standing by ready for use rather than sale. It is more like a compact country garden than a plant emporium in a floating city. Inside the two tunnels inherent Italian style and design meets good horticulture and all the plants are arranged in an inviting and inspiring display, by association and height rather than plant groups as in almost all British garden centres.

Dogs sauntered easily amongst customers and the staff offer knowledgeable bits of advice and suggestions like good hosts. Indeed, there is more than a whiff of a cocktail party or a gallery opening about the atmosphere, regulars greeting each other and catching up on family news, introducing partners and friends as they compare the

OPPOSITE – *The garden centre of Laguna Fiorita is small and squeezed in a patch of ground below the campanile of Chiesa dell'Abbazia della Misericordia. But it is packed with plants of high quality.*

worthiness of this geranium or that hydrangea. One woman I spoke to said she had come here from Marghera where she had space for a garden and visited regularly as part of a day out to the city. But it seemed that most were locals looking for colour for a window box or balcony. There was none of the bulk buying that characterises the average out-of-town British garden centre with loaded trolleys and car boots being stacked with plants. The shoppers arrive and leave on foot and the baskets were small and easily carried away. It was the difference between doing the weekly shop at a supermarket and visiting the local market for something delicious.

The nursery is towered over by the bell tower of the early fourteenth-century Scuola della Misericordia. Whereas most citizens had no access to any kind of involvement in the government of their affairs, the Scuola represented and expected involvement from the professional classes, those not noble nor wealthy enough to be part of the government bodies such as the council of Ten or the Signoria but with sufficient resources to endow these scuole with fine buildings and works of art and to play a charitable role to these members in need. The Scuola della Misericordia is the most complete surviving example; being crammed in between towers and houses and the remnants of former buildings all adds to the sense of an oasis, a refuge bubbling green life up into the stone, brick and water of the city.

Before I left I indulged myself by slipping behind the scenes to admire the shredders, hoists, mowers and ranks of stacked wheelbarrows. I love the behind-the-scenes working areas of all busy gardens although I do not usually associate this entirely practical world with an urban garden centre. But just as I was about to go a boat arrived disgorging half a dozen workers, coming back for lunch with saws, spades and the paraphernalia of working gardeners. It turns out that the nursery does a great deal of maintenance and landscaping right across the lagoon, hence the amount of well-used kit and the enormous heap of waste material accumulated from client's gardens.

It was an insight into the Italian attitude towards gardening compared to the British. In Britain, garden centres, and to a lesser extent nurseries, are places where gardeners go to buy plants and materials to enable them to garden, in the same way that Italians go to a food market to buy ingredients for them to cook. But here, at Laguna Fiorita, was a place that looked good, had an entirely approachable, friendly culture, made shopping an enjoyable social occasion but also provided the labour and expertise to look after your plants and garden so that you, the customer, could appreciate and enjoy the beauty of the plants yet completely bypass the business of actually gardening.

OPPOSITE – *Laguna Fiorita is the base for the team of gardeners that work all over the city and their tools are stored in and amongst the plant sales.*

San Francesco della Vigna

It has been oft remarked that the different sestieri of Venice are remarkably self-contained and separate from each other, with locals spending much of their lives happily within the bounds of their own small area of the city, regarding other sestieri with suspicion or even hostility. Despite the modern global world, where every airport, chain hotel and shopping mall vies to belong to the same amorphous nowhere, this fine-tuned individuality within the coherent Venetian identity is still apparent.

Your boat glides east in the basin past the Piazzetta and the Palazzo Ducale, leaving behind the flow of trudging tourists on the Riva degli Schiavoni, then it turns left into Rio della Pietà and as you enter the most eastern sestiere of Castello, you sense a change. It is another place.

Castello – once a distinct island amongst the many – was originally known as Isola di Olivolo and was the first to be settled in the lagoon. A castle was built on it and from thence came the name Castello. It is best known for the Arsenale, which, since it was founded at the beginning of the twelfth century, was the engine room of the Republic's high days of power and trade but, amongst its many treasures, it also has the highest proportion of permanent residents than any of the other five sestieri.

The outward signs are subtle. More clothes hang on lines strung outside windows overlooking the canal. There are fewer tourists shops – indeed, fewer shops of any kind – and more of the sturdy metal Venetian barrows and trolleys laden with vegetables, fridges or boxes of loo paper. Old men sit in cheap chairs reading the paper, ignoring our barge as it chugs by. Backpacked children trudge to school across the bridges, and dogs sniff and head off as though called on sudden urgent business.

You moor and pass under tall columns supporting an elevated gallery into Campo San Francesco della Vigna, with the church of San Francesco della Vigna and surrounding buildings glowing pink, apricot and golden stucco in the morning light. San Francesco della Vigna is one of two Franciscan churches in Venice – the other is the fourteenth-century Santa Maria Gloriosa dei Frari in San Polo, the biggest church in the city. San Francesco della Vigna was designed by Jacopo Sansovino after he had been appointed public architect, and was built between 1534 and 1554 at the height of the flurry of building deliberately trying to create Venice as a rival to Rome in beauty and power.

OPPOSITE – *The vineyard is recently planted but uses the old-fashioned technique of training the vines vertically up poles. The monastery's campanile – one of the tallest in the city and where the bell peals for the start and end of Lent – towers above.*

However, Sansovino died in 1538 and San Francesco della Vigna's white marble facade was designed by Andrea Palladio. This was the first of Palladio's Venetian commissions (although it was actually completed after the subsequent commission of the church of San Giorgio Maggiore). The campanile, one of Venice's tallest, was completed by 1581 and its bell tolls the end of Lent and the beginning of Carnival.

Entering the monastery buildings to one side of the church, you pass through two cloisters charged with light softly falling on stone. A door takes you out into a large, open space flanked by colonnaded ambulatories on two sides. Half cloister, half garden. In fact, more than just a garden because this was originally the site of the largest vineyard in Venice and there has been continuous wine production there, starting when the island was first occupied and continuing after the monastery's founding in the thirteenth century.

Half the area is grassed and has rows of posts, each supporting a vine, looking like serried ranks of closed beach umbrellas. The vines are being raised on a sixteenth-century system and were only planted in 2018 by Santa Margherita Wines, who are also raising the vines in return for helping with the restoration of the ruined chapel of San Marco within the monastery.

The grapes were once the famous Venetian 'Fragola' variety, much feted for their distinctive strawberry flavour, but are now replaced with 'Glera'. These are similarly fragrant and sweetish but used to make prosecco and, although originating in Slovenia, have been grown in the Veneto, where their Venetian provenance has been fiercely protected for over five hundred years.

The vines of the monastery take up less than half the area but are set to make over two thousand bottles, all of which will be given away. The second vineyard, in another courtyard, backed by the rear of the church and modern flats, produces about a thousand bottles. The proceeds from the sale of the wine helps finance scholarships for students at the Institute of Ecumenical Studies, which is part of the modern monastic complex. It is clearly a marketing gift for the wine company and a much-needed source of support for the monastery. Everyone is happy.

I was shown round by Father Stefano. He was a grave, gentle presence with a modern face that meant his Franciscan habit had something of the historical costume about it, like a Beefeater's or Papal Guard's, and I noticed jeans showing beneath the hem of his brown woollen frock. He has lived here for 35 years but is now only one of the six remaining monks. By the end of the sixteenth century, Venice had over 30 monasteries and the same number of convents, amounting to around 3,000 monks and nuns.

OPPOSITE – *Pillars support an elevated gallery leading to the campo in front of the Friary.*

THIS PAGE – *This was once the largest vineyard in Venice but now most of it is grassed over with just a few vines remaining in production.*

Francesco della Vigna once had more than 150 monks in the order and needed the large vegetable garden that formerly took up half of the current vineyard. But this has now been reduced to a small, albeit abundant, plot growing tomatoes, aubergines, peppers, celery, chard, parsley and basil, with a few fruit trees, four large olive trees that provide the monks' supply of olive oil and this new vineyard.

A long, sunken boathouse cuts into the area, the water of the lagoon pushed up its steps and under the doors as large boats pass the other side of the garden wall. In the calm seclusion of the vineyard, it is a reminder that nothing and nowhere in Venice is ever far away from the water.

In 1880 the buildings around a further cloister burnt down and a large gas holder was built on the site. Another was added in 1928. They are no longer in use but a large crane set inside the rusting skeleton of one was beginning to turn it into luxury flats. When complete, it will almost certainly, like so many buildings and apartments in twenty-first-century Venice, be used for holiday lets, Airbnb or second homes.

Having shown me round the vineyard, which makes for a fairly brief visit, Father Stefano opened a bottle of the 2017 vintage and at nine in the morning we took a glass each. For all his gravitas and Franciscan modesty, he drank his with admirable relish, and rightly so. It was delicious.

THIS PAGE – *In 1880 the buildings around a further cloister burnt down and large gas holders replaced them. They are no longer in use but the rusting skeleton of one is being turned into luxury apartments.*

THIS PAGE — *Father Stefano, monk and vintner.*

Palazzo Contarini dal Zaffo

Our barge carefully slips past the boats parked along the canal, the Fondamenta della Sensa, a sidewalk to the Rio de la Sensa. There is an ambling, unhurried activity, coffee being drunk, children lagging and dragging until promised ice creams, dogs on leads. Three upright nuns in white habits stride, overtaking the dawdlers and us on our boat. Workshops opening onto the water mend small craft and others, still proclaiming their ownership and trade in fading lettering, are overgrown with plants.

Cannaregio, although become trendy, still resists being swamped by tourism, still evinces a sense of self and identity. As a tourist, this is the Venice you can imagine absorbing you, imagine becoming an instant local, folding into the *sestieri*. Utter delusion, of course.

We are on our way, circuitously, to Palazzo Contarini dal Zaffo, where there is a garden that was once famed as much for its guests as its horticulture. In its far corner is a square building, a chimney stack in each corner and two of its walls rising out of the northern lagoon, just across the marina from the nursery at Laguna Fiorita. This is the Casino degli Spiriti or Casino of the Spirits, referring not to any ghostly activity but to the eminence of the 'spirits' that used to assemble there in the fifteenth and sixteenth centuries for conversation and spirited company. Amongst their number was the poet Pietro Aretino and his friend the painter Titian, who lived nearby on the Fondamente Nove. (His contemporary, Tintoretto, lived just a stone's throw away on the Fondamenta dei Mori, but there is no record of this rougher, less sophisticated but no-less-talented artist being part of any intellectual clique or polite society.)

A century later, the casino was embellished and decorated by Tiepolo, amongst others, and still retained its role as a meeting place for those wishing to discuss the arts or latest ideas.

To reach this building, the distinguished visitors had to walk right through the garden that ran from the palazzo on Rio Madonna dell'Orto out to the sea. The house was built for Cardinal Gasparo Contarini at the beginning of the sixteenth century. The Contarini were one of the great patrician families of Venice and Gasparo was a diplomat and senator before, in 1535, despite having no ecclesiastical training or experience, the Farnese Pope, Paul III, made him a cardinal and Bishop of Belluno expressly to harness his diplomatic skills in dealing with the rise of Protestantism in northern Europe. He died in 1542 at the age of 59.

At one time this garden was famed as being one of the best in Venice although now, while still large, with good trees and superb views out across to the islands of

Murano and San Michele, it has lost its Renaissance structure and coherence. However, large pedimented doorways lead to low-slung modern buildings and long pathways still remain where they once were, but instead of being part of the formality and balance of the original sixteenth-century garden, they now border a random mixture of trees and shrubs. It is clearly loved and used but it is as though no-one is quite aware of what lies beneath the garden's twenty-first-century skin.

A painting by Francesco Guardi, made in the late 1770s and now in the Art Institute of Chicago, shows a parterre made from *plats* of grass lined with judiciously spaced rose bushes. On the wide gravel or beaten sand paths, bewigged men in frock-coats escort bonnetted ladies in full gowns and dresses. The lagoon fades palely away to the north and the casino has, adding a surprisingly domestic touch to the otherwise stately scene, washing hanging from its windows.

A watercolour by the same artist from the same period in the Ashmolean in Oxford, drawn from a boat in the lagoon, shows the casino and garden walls as slightly dilapidated, in need of repair. So perhaps the the garden was already slipping away by then, its days of sparkling repartee and creativity long past, and the very simplistic depiction in the painting over-fanciful.

In any event it was certainly dilapidated by the beginning of the twentieth century and was remade rather than restored, its English owners using an English idiom.. In the 1950s, the garden was apparently the setting for elaborate and glamorous society parties.

Well, no more. The garden has been doubly institutionalised since being shared with Casa Cardinal Piazza, a Christian guesthouse that has the section of the garden closest to the Palazzo. There is something of the public park in this part of the garden, although the ghost of the former garden with its parties and distinguished poets, painters and thinkers making their way through it can still be felt within the remaining brick walls, if not the planting.

Beyond a dividing wall is the Casino of the Spirits – albeit now buttressed with additional low buildings around it like bulbils – and the original and still-functioning vegetable garden, with a bower covered with a Venetian 'Fragola' vine that belongs to the Nunnery of the Daughters of Divine Providence. But beyond the cultivation of the vegetables in a few raised beds, both the potential and the history of this part of the garden lie submerged beneath a suppressing mulch of gentle reverence.

NEXT PAGE – *The garden wall, with its statues balanced high on stone columns, bounds onto the lagoon with views across to Murano and the cemetery at San Michele.*

OPPOSITE – *At one time the garden was a meeting place for writers, painters and poets but now it has been divided into two parts, Casa Cardinal Piazza, a Christian guest house, and a nursing home run by nuns of Divine Providence. But despite institutionalisation, the ghosts of literary soirees can still be sensed.*

Giardino Mistico

The magnificently operatic high-Baroque marble facade of the church of the Scalzi sits on the Grand Canal, next door to the railways station. It dates from the 1670s and was the church of the monastery of the Discalced Carmelites. Despite conjuring up an image akin to defurring a kettle, this refers to their practice of going barefoot – which gives the Italian word Scalzi. The barefoot Carmelites were a branch of the order founded in the sixteenth century by St Teresa of Avila, dedicated to an austere devotion based upon absolute poverty. The Carmelite monastery had a large garden, including a vineyard, where they grew all their own vegetables as well as being a physical and spiritual sanctuary from the world and heavily symbolic of the garden of Eden and Paradise. Whereas the *Paradeiza* of Islam were a place of rest and ease from labour, the monastic tradition assiduously cultivated as much of their land as possible and saw dignity and spiritual restitution in tending them.

Under the French Napoleonic rule between 1805 and 1814, religious orders in Venice were suppressed and disbanded and the Scalzi monastery became a glass factory for much of the nineteenth century. The creation of the station and houses for workers in the 1860s took away half the garden, which, as the guide books say, 'used to stretch to platform 5'. The friars returned at the end of the nineteenth century and up until the 1960s there were 70 friars, but that is now down to just five.

But the garden, although much reduced, is still large. Despite the railway station on the other side of a high wall and the busy boat traffic on the Grand Canal in the front, it is also extraordinarily quiet and completely hidden. The garden was completely redesigned and remade in 2014 based upon St Teresa's book *The Interior Castle* published in 1577, three years before her death. This laid out seven mansions or stages in the mystical progress towards union with God.

So the Mystic garden is designed, as is the Italian wont, by an architect, Giorgio Forti, who trained in Venice under Carlo Scarpa. In the extensive literature written by the architectural team describing the garden they say,

The goal was to make the garden into a sort of innovative catechism for the modern world. Through a reading of nature and its symbolism, the aim was to reflect the content of the Catholic religion and specific features of the Order of the Discalced Carmelites, which has been profoundly linked with Christian mysticism since its very foundation.

Thus it is divided into seven distinct areas. The first, nearest to the monastic buildings and the church, is an area of mown lawn representing the one integral existence from which all things are made. Although slightly crushed under the weight of this symbolism it is a perfectly pleasant if unremarkable square of mown grass.

THIS PAGE — *The herb beds are edged with railways sleepers fixed with railway spikes, which is a nod to the railway station next door just the other side of the monastery walls.*

(Disclaimer: It has to be said that Italians, especially Italian architects, just love this sort of thing. They love it much more than gardens. So, in so much as this is a very Italian and Venetian garden, it is right and proper to take it seriously. But it has to be said that this British gardener feels a little uncomfortable ...)

The next stage or section is a garden of Simples, or a physic garden with nine beds edged with railway sleepers held in place – a nice touch – by railway spikes. The beds containing the herbs and plants that every monastery grew to use as medicines. This knowledge and faith in plant medicines, often gathered growing wild as well as grown in gardens, spread right across society until remarkably recently. I remember the old lady that we bought our farmhouse from in 1990, who had been born there in 1919, telling us 'When my mother wanted medicines she went to the hedgerow bank outside the kitchen window'.

One of the nine beds – larger than the others – was filled with just one herb –*Melissa moldovica*. This special species of lemon balm is the ingredient from which the monks here have been distilling a potion – aqua di Melissa – since 1710 that is used as an antispasmodic and still widely sold and dispensed.

The third section is for vegetables grown in long temporary raised beds divided by black membrane. It is completely practical, and productive without any nod towards a potager-like decorative quality. The gardener in me loved the rows of superb chicory – not least because the Veneto is the spiritual home of chicory. The amount of vegetables here far exceed the possible needs of the five friars that remain and their available labour – the garden is maintained by a local nursery – and the majority of it provides income by being sold at the local farmer's market.

The next stage of the spiritual process is a small vineyard filled with the various vines of Venice and the Veneto. There are more vine paths festooning the hugely long pergolas that flank the length of both sides of the garden. The monastery, under the auspices of the Consorzio Vini Venezia, produces over 600 bottles of wine a year. There is a cross path dividing the vegetable plot from the vineyard with a large pomegranate in the very centre and a brick wall doubling as a seat encircling it. The pomegranate serves as a symbol of fertility, health, longevity and luck amongst other things, all good, and appears in a number of religions as an integral practical and symbolic component in gardens.

After the vineyard comes an orchard with apples, figs, cherries, apricots, peaches, persimmons. There was one particularly luscious black fig that called to me as I wandered around. I had never seen a fig that looked so ripe, so absolutely ready to be eaten and finally I could resist it no more and guiltily took it and bit deep. It turned out to be profoundly disappointing – unripe and rather woolly and insipid. Somehow that made the sense of guilt of pilfering fruit from such a self-consciously holy place all the worse.

THIS PAGE — *As well as a small vineyard, vines are trained over pergolas running down the the full length of either side of the long garden.*

The penultimate, sixth section is an olive grove of thirteen large trees representing Christ and the twelve apostles, and the olive itself as a symbol of wisdom. Olive oil is duly processed from their harvest.

Finally, following St Teresa's seven mansions of the soul, you come to what she describes as The Wood, although it takes a leap of imagination and generosity to call the few trees huddled against the end wall a wood. The generosity is in part needed for their paucity but also for the limitations of the site because their main practical purpose is to screen an ugly modern building. It is an unlikely mix, horticulturally at least, with tamarisk, weeping willow, a Judas tree, a cedar of Lebanon, a palm and an evergreen oak but there is an (elaborate) explanation for each choice.

There is a long tradition of gardens having symbolic journeys and meanings woven into their structure and planting but I have never visited one that is so determinedly based upon a text.

The garden is beautifully put together, well maintained and extremely impressive. It has that air of something thrust into the world, as though blinking in the glare of daylight and its strict brief and parameters mean that some parts work better than others, as per a garden. It needs time to settle so it can become what it wants to be perhaps despite, rather than because of, its rigid brief.

One last thing. For the record, the charming Carmelite brother who kindly showed us around was fully and robustly shod.

THIS PAGE — *Herbs creating building blocks against the backdrop of the vine arch and high walls.*

Giardini Papadopoli

Down at the far western end of the Grand Canal Santa Croce, past the railway station and under the disconcerting modernity of Calatrava's Ponte della Costituzione, are imposing iron gates and high walls over which tall trees tower. This is the Giardini Papadopoli, a small but – at the right time – charming park. I have visited in September when, after a long hot summer, it is parched and tired and like all weather-worn public spaces is a little dispiriting and has little to offer other than shade. But visit in spring and it is a glowing green delight, bright with flower. The visitor may be picky about these things but Venetians enjoy and use it greatly.

It was made in 1834 on land that once belonged to a monastery of the Poor Clare nuns. This Franciscan order lost their land in 1810 when Napoleon swept away the Venetian monasteries at the beginning of the nineteenth century. It was duly bought by the Papadopoli family who were wealthy merchants that had moved from the Venetian colony of Corfu at the end of the eighteenth century and in 1834 Count Spiridione Papadopoli commissioned a garden in the 'English Style', eschewing the European formality and using the landscaping language of Brown and Repton to make a garden with glades, winding paths, a small lake and two small hills made from the spoil of the lake. It had borders with a collection of exotic plants that plant hunters were increasingly gathering from around the world. There was also an aviary with exotic birds such as silver pheasants and parrots.

It was damaged by bombing in the First World War but restored and, rather like the Giardini Reali, and opened to the public in the 1920s before being reduced in size by over a third in 1933 when the Rio Novo canal and Piazzale Roma were built.

What remains is a public space with a calm, peaceful atmosphere that is a solace from the bustle of the railway and bus stations, the crowded streets and even the business of the canals. The maturity of the trees, many from the original planting, does not just cast a cool shade but also a sense of tranquility. In this very watery place many groups of tall trees add a deeper connection to Earth than Venice can often offer.

There is bright colour from the brilliant yellow violas in circular beds and the last remnants of red tulips, the petals falling as I watch, as well as a series of crimson, pink and white azaleas. This is a place that people visit rather than use as a leafy detour on any journey. It leads to nowhere but is a destination, albeit not for so many that its becomes crowded. People take their lunch, read papers or sit sprawled unselfconsciously in each other's laps.

In this city where water dominates everything, including all transport that sustains life, it is not surprising to find a large statue to a hydraulic engineer. Pietro Paleocapa, was responsible for a range of works in the mid-nineteenth century on the Brenta river, the Malamocco dam and, away from Venice, played a significant role in designing the Suez Canal.

THIS PAGE – *The garden is one of the few public spaces in Venice where the city can momentarily be set aside amongst the maturity of its superb trees.*

Water and Bridges

One of the strangest things about Venice is not so much the presence of water as the absence of roads and road traffic. Machines have not overridden human connection in the way that they do the minute anyone gets behind the wheel of a car. Boatmen talk and call to each other and gondoliers shout a warning 'oi' as they round a corner rather blast a horn. The water softens what sound there is too, rather than bouncing it back against the walls as tarmac does. There is, of course, the sound of motor engines from the 2,000-odd licensed motor boats but all are subject to strict speed restrictions, so the engines never scream or roar.

There are 170 different canals winding through the city, extending to just short of 100km, all tidal, rising and falling a metre or more twice a day so frequently you step easily into a boat going out to dinner and have to half climb, half jump up to the landing point on your return a few hours later.

THIS PAGE — *Nothing symbolises Venice more precisely than the silhouette of a gondola.*

THIS PAGE – *The canals bounce back every shifting beam breaking through the clouds and reflect every building. This adds a depth and richness to the fabric of the city that is not matched anywhere else.*

NEXT PAGE – *A Mascareto boat off the Zattere with the Redentore church across the water on the Giudecca.*

Without bridges the city really would be a maze for travellers on foot and as it is it certainly feels labyrinthian. There are over 450 bridges, ranging from the biggest and most famous of them all, the Rialto, to little brick arches. It is a city of bridges as much as a city of canals. Many are brick, some majestically of stone and a few, like the Accademia Bridge, of wood, but all connect the city like links in a chain. However, the sheer number and frequency of them mean that any walk involves innumerable rises and falls, creating a strangely unfamiliar pedestrian experience, like walking across fields of ridge and furrow.

THIS PAGE – *The canal entrance of Palazzo Gradenigo with water coming under the door.*

OPPOSITE TOP – *There are a few major arterial canals but most are surprisingly small, the veins that feed into the recesses of the city.*

OPPOSITE BOTTOM – *Spend any time in a small boat and you will find yourself ducking and bobbing underneath the arches of bridges, often terrifyingly low, into the recesses of the city.*

THIS PAGE – *The bridge of Riva dei Sette Martiri, near the Biennale Gardens.*

THIS PAGE – *The buildings rise sheer from the water, not on it but in it, of it, and perhaps ultimately returning to it.*

OPPOSITE – *The passing* ferro *or prow of a gondola, said to replicate the beak of a Roman galley.*

Palazzetto Bru Zane

Bang in the centre of San Polo, at the heart of the bulge of city contained by the arcing curve of the Grand Canal where San Polo and Santa Croce rub against each other, is the Centre de Musique Romantique Française housed in the Palazzetto Bru Zane. It is not easy to find. Twist and wind through the streets, double back, try again, and at last you find the brass nameplate and through the door into one of Venice's most charming gardens.

In itself there is nothing so very exceptional. But it sits easy with itself. It has poise and proportion and the planting, although simple, is subtle and immensely pleasing. It originally linked the Palazzo Zane (now the Scuola Livio Sanudo) to an ornate casino built at the end of the seventeenth century as a theatre and concert hall housing about 100 people for private performances for the Zane family. This casino, or *palazzetto*, was extensively restored in 2007 by the Fondation Bru and the garden laid out anew by Camilla Zanarotti.

The door opens onto a path that ducks you under the green weeping branches of a mulberry, past waist-high walls into a small paved courtyard with wellhead. The high walls of the buildings are a peachy pink stucco or the faded terracotta of bare brick, and both are perfect compliment to the intense green of spring foliage. There is a lot of green: ivy, yew, *Fatsia Japonica*, a huge cypress and the mulberry, all a rich deep emerald. The palazzetto is smothered in wisteria and a huge white rose covers a three-storey pink side wall. We focus our horticultural attention on plants and the colours of their flowers but this garden exemplifies how important is the background colour of the wall that any climber ascends and these soft pinks and terracottas are perfect.

The paved yard has a table and a few chairs and enough shade around the edges to take or leave the sun as one wills. A tall and unusually elegant olive adds a silvery tone to the pastel palette. The proportions are just so and immediately it feels a space to sit and read in or just listen to the cello seeping from the windows above.

A couple of steps flanked by a pair of putti and a low yew hedge above the retaining wall go up to a little daisy-speckled lawn with a backdrop of tall fatsia completely cladding the wall out onto the calle behind. A bushy fig and pittosporum bulge and flow against the tightly clipped yew hedges. There are a few *Iris Japonica* in the borders but this is not a flower garden. Green leaves, beautiful soft orange brick, the grey of the paving and painted stucco harmonise as sweetly and simply as the chamber music, no doubt nineteenth century and French, pouring out into the garden from the rehearsal rooms within.

OPPOSITE – *Roses spilling from the wall amongst the confident and rich simplicity of the planting of Palazzetto Bru Zane.*

THIS PAGE — *The garden is really just a simple courtyard, once connecting the palazzo with its seventeenth-century music hall. The palazzo has disappeared but the garden has a balance and elegance that remains.*

THIS PAGE — *A couple of steps flanked by a pair of putti and a low yew hedge above the retaining wall spilling over with a capping of ivy go up to a little daisy-speckled lawn.*

THIS PAGE – *Sit for more than a few minutes in the courtyard and you will hear through the windows of the rehearsal rooms, the drifting sound of nineteenth-century chamber music pouring sweetly out into the garden.*

Palazzo Soranzo Cappello

The Fondamenta Gradenigo alongside Rio Marin links the two necks of the Grand Canal as it bulges around the sestrieri of San Polo and Santa Croce and you arrive at the gates of Palazzo Gradenigo. The high garden wall next to it belongs to Palazzo Soranzo Cappello. The Gradenigo and Soranzo houses have been in close proximity for centuries and a Gradenigo doge who died in 1311 was followed by Giovanni Soranzo less than a year later. Both are old and noble Venetian families with old and noble palazzos next door to each other and both with notable gardens. But that is where, in the twenty-first century at least, the similarities end.

In medieval times this was an area of vegetable gardens and fields where dyed cloth was laid out to dry. When palazzi such as Gradenigo and Soranzo Cappello were built in the fifteenth and seventeenth centuries they had large gardens attached to them. Until the early twentieth century the area of Santa Croce on the other side of the Grand Canal opposite the railway station still had large gardens as well a park that stretched along the Grand Canal with avenues where, in this floating city of shoulder-width calles and canals barely wide enough for two gondolas to pass, riders and carriages could parade. Then in the 1920s Mussolini built blocks of apartments to house railway workers and the park and gardens disappeared or were dramatically reduced. However, the garden of Palazzo Soranzo Cappello remained entire.

Palazzo Soranzo Cappello is now another imposing facade on a side canal. Venice is heavy with buildings like these. But in its day, it was feted not just as a fine and grand palace but also for its especially fine and grand garden. The garden reached its heyday in the early eighteenth century and apart from some alterations made at the beginning of the twentieth century remained largely unaltered but became increasingly neglected.

It was the setting for Henry James's *The Aspern Papers* where the air of the palazzo and its grounds is one of impoverished but stylish decay. The garden is described by the narrator as having 'weeds and its rough, wild tangle, its sweet characteristic shabbiness'. However, he quickly hires a gardener who – with narrative neatness but improbable horticultural speed – manages to produce enough cut flowers with which to bombard the elderly occupant and her niece. With this information and our knowledge of the horticultural tastes of the 1880s it shows that there were cultivated and tended flowerbeds amongst the bowers and 'fragrant alleys'.

OPPOSITE – *Looking through the courtyard with its flanking citrus trees and wild flower meadow down to the loggia at the far end of the garden.*

But fiction allows any amount of liberties to tell a tale. There is no way of knowing what the garden of Soranzo Cappello was actually like when James was living in and writing about Venice. In any event there are few flower beds there now and little or no cultivation of any sort. The ghost of its eighteenth-century garden remains but this is now heavily overlaid with the very twenty-first-century conceit of benign, creative neglect.

The garden is designed to be entered from the house. As with all Venetian palazzo's, this means arriving by boat from the Rio, passing through a long, large androne with the familiar pink and cream diamond tiles, handsome and grand but also able to take a regular flooding, on through double glass doors with huge grilled gates and out to a broad path running down the middle of an enclosed courtyard. The path is flanked by lemons in pots and four small lawns, underplanted with spring bulbs. In early May most were over but there remained the almost black 'Queen of Night' tulips and bluebells dotted amongst the ears of the foxtail barley.

Around the edge of this courtyard, inset into niches in the wall, are statues of the eleven first Roman emperors plus Julius Caesar. These have been here since at least 1709 as there is an engraving from that date featuring them. It struck me that there was something slightly odd about these statues and when I looked closer I realised that they all shared the same bull-necked and double-chinned face, quite unlike most classical statues and distinctly, almost perversely, unflattering. I like to think that the man who commissioned them was similarly stoutly built and that this is his likeness confirming an ancestral connection to these great Romans.

The central path leads to steps flanked by huge statues of Hercules wrestling Antaeus, in a very similar fashion both in position and execution to the entrance into the garden from the courtyard at Palazzo Malipiero. I have always related to poor Antaeus, son of the earth goddess Gaia, whose strength derived from his contact with the mother earth and was defeated by being eventually lifted up and held clear of the ground so, thus weakened, was crushed to death by the thug Hercules. This story often pops up in Italian garden statuary and is perhaps symbolic of the relationship to gardens and the natural world, with the hero defeating someone with a deep connection to the earth by brute strength.

OPPOSITE – *The courtyard is surrounded by eighteenth-century statues of Roman emperors in alcoves. All have the same, rather full, face and bull neck and are probably based upon the likeness of the man who commissioned them.*

Beyond this courtyard the garden crosses mown lawn and moves into gradual and deliberate decay and disarray, albeit entirely deliberate and cleverly conceived and executed. The original parterres and divisions are marked with grass, swathes of liriope, a mass of irises, and thousands of spring bulbs including a great square of *Allium ursinum*, wild garlic, channelling its invasive tendencies into a superb mass of floating white flower.

Giuseppe Rallo has been in charge of the restoration of the garden since 2005 when the palazzo became the new headquarters of the State Office for Historical Monuments of Venice and the Veneto.

He explained to me the philosophy behind the garden's restoration. The intention is to accept decay as part of natural change and to allow it to continue and be part of the story of the garden. To that end ground elder and bindweed romp unchecked. Some trees, such as the hackberry, *Celtis australis*, have been encouraged to grow tall to screen the modern buildings on one side of the garden. Others have been cleared and cut back to let in more light but the paper mulberry, *Broussonetia*, and bay, *Laurus nobilis*, have both been allowed to seed freely, with saplings popping up through the irises and massed agapanthus leaves – both of which must look wonderful in their season. A statue, the only survivor from the original double row that lined the central path, remains half buried and horizontal in the sea of ivy around it.

At the far end of the garden is a large loggia with its tympanum supported by eight pillars. This grand and impressive structure is almost inappropriately formal amongst the horticultural shabby-chic around it. That is, of course, the desired effect and one must make of that what you will. But the longer I spent in the garden – and I visited in late summer and the following spring – it seemed that it had been overtaken not so much by the untrammelled spirit of change expressing itself in liberated and random growth, but a design conceit, in itself as mannered and controlled as any formal parterre. Having said that, James's novella is based upon the idea of romantic ageing and decay and lost dreams, which is exactly in tune with the enduring notion of Venice as a city.

THIS PAGE – *White bearded irises flowering beneath the vine trellis in the Brolo.*

THIS PAGE & OPPOSITE — *The garden at Soranzo Cappello is an exercise in marrying horticultural control and abandon. So the climbing roses are carefully pruned and trained up the brick pillar whilst beneath them plants, including some that conventional gardeners might think of as 'weeds', are allowed to grow unfettered. In the Brolo, formerly the vegetable and fruit garden for the palazzo, shrub roses are encouraged to billow and spill , growing out of the meadow planting beneath them.*

Around the side of the palazzo is the 'Brolo', the area traditionally occupied by the vegetable garden and orchard in large Venetian gardens. In spring the long covered walkway drips with wisteria flowers and the end furthest from the fondamenta wall has a vine growing over a pergola underplanted with irises of an astonishingly rich purple. There are no vegetables now, but a large clump of roses rises from the grass which is dotted with perennials such as aquilegias and the foliage of spring bulbs now passed.

Like the rest of the garden this almost works, is almost lovely but feels like a good idea that has not – yet – become a good garden. Much of this is practical. The garden has apparently been made and is run on a very limited budget. But there is also limited enthusiasm for gardening as part of the sustained development of a garden. The Italian sensibility is much more attracted to a garden as a concept rather than mundane horticultural practicalities.

The truth is that the garden is greatly cared for and greatly admired – just not gardened very much. And however lofty your horticultural concepts might be, you cannot have a garden without gardening. This can be done with a very light touch and there is as much skill in knowing when not to do things as when to interfere – but as a gardener, I longed to roll up my sleeves and interfere.

THIS PAGE – *The loggia, supported by eight large columns, is very grand and would have been the culmination of the eighteenth-century formal garden, whereas now it rises up out of a carefully contrived twenty-first-century wild garden.*

Palazzo Gradenigo

A few steps along from Soranzo Cappello, the Fondamenta Gradenigo in Santa Croce comes to an end at a rather grand stone arch that leads into a small courtyard with private steps down to the Rio Marin. A doorway, slightly ajar, is directly ahead, revealing a flood-worn pink-and-ivory pastellone floor gleaming faintly in the darkness within. Set into the wall along the fondamenta, before you enter the courtyard, is a locked metal gate leading to a gravel path curving between vine-covered walls and blending into the rich wash of a tantalisingly green garden.

This is Palazzo Gradenigo.

It was, like its neighbour, originally set in large grounds stretching as far as the Grand Canal, with pavilions and stables for 30 horses. In 1782, the garden hosted a bullfight in honour of the future Tsar of Russia, Paul I, and his wife. It remained the largest private garden in Venice until Mussolini confiscated most of it in the 1920s to build blocks of flats for railway workers. What is left is barely one-tenth of the original plot but, in Venetian terms at least, it still has a sizeable garden.

The Gradenigos were amongst the 24 founding families of the Republic and were a recurrent name through its greatest years. They were grand, with four Gradenigo doges, and the palazzo is suitably large to accommodate that status, although by the time it was built, in the middle of the seventeenth century, the Gradenigos' star was, like that of so many of the Venetian mercantile aristocracy, on the wane.

By the time the current owner, Toto Bergamo Rossi, President of Venetian Heritage, first came to the house in 1999, it was partitioned into a large number of shabby flats and the garden had become a lumber yard. As well as restoring the palazzo, reducing the apartments and keeping the beautifully furnished piano nobile for himself, he tackled the garden. This was a very un-Venetian thing to do, indeed, an un-Italian thing. The average Italian, in a similar position, would get someone in, in the same way as we might get someone to lay a patio or put up a garden fence. But Toto became personally engaged – engrossed – by the project. Despite having no experience or indeed any previous interest, he set about clearing and completely remodelling and planting the garden, becoming increasingly, by his own admission, obsessed with the garden and gardening.

THIS PAGE – *An iron gate leading to Fondamenta Gradenigo holds a tantalising glimpse of the garden of Palazzo Gradenigo.*

NEXT PAGE – *The vine-covered dining area, entered from the palazzo at one end and with steps leading down to the lawn.*

Clearly, not many Venetians have the opportunity to garden, so I asked Toto if his new-found discovery of the pleasures of gardening was atypical for the modern Italian. He thought that this was very much the case. 'Italy has forgotten how to garden,' he told me. 'Almost no Italians visit the great gardens. Only Tuscany has any modern garden traditions.' Whilst this is obviously a generalisation, my experience of visiting gardens all over Italy bears it out. It also shows how the deep-seated regionalism Italy still holds – in what other country would people refer to a part of the same country just 240km (150 miles) away with such broad cultural definition?

The result of Toto's obsession and hard work is deceptively simple, albeit meticulously designed and maintained. He has made the garden into an outdoor salon, with a central lawn like a carpet domed with a gnarled and sizeable weeping Japanese pagoda tree, *Sophora japonica*, planted in 1923. Around the lawn is a gravel path and around the path, against the walls of the house and the high boundary wall that screens off the garden of Soranzo Cappello, is a ribbon of narrow beds.

While lawns are commonplace in any British garden, and thus unremarkable, a Venetian lawn is a trophy because the scorching summer sun and the saltwater that floods in with the acqua alta mean that any grass in Venice struggles to survive, let alone thrive. The velvety striped green of the lawn is therefore a statement of extravagant, even indulgent, luxury, generously laid out on the ground. The gravel path is for taking a turn around the garden, admiring the flowers on the one side and the grass on the other. The climbers on the garden walls are, Toto says, like tapestries in a room, shifting in colour throughout the seasons but constant in their cladding.

The path along the lawn on the furthest side from the house continues on past a second bower, overhung with pomegranates like Christmas baubles and buffered along the edges by shrubs. This cleverly extends the garden down to a gate onto the Ramo de le Chioverette and Mussolini's railway workers' apartments, and is like a long, thin garden entire unto itself, a horticultural calle, rather than just a functional narrow path leading out to the back gate. A small thing, but the mark of a good and clever designer.

At one end of the lawn, entered from the house and screened from the fondamenta by a wall, is a raised dining area beneath a vine-covered pergola. At the other end is a matching arbour, this time clad in a voluminous wisteria. These are ordered, stately spaces, touched with formality in what is a deliberately soft and informal garden. Yet they are not private in the same way that a British back garden is a personal, private domain. The palazzo has apartments that can be rented and guests can use and enjoy the garden along with the exquisite entrance hall, stairs and other communal areas. The garden is for sharing with a select few, whilst the rest of the world just catches a moment of green harmony through the bars of the metal gate leading from the fondamenta, or perhaps glimpsed from a boat as they pass. Above all, it is this combination of beguiling glimpses and exclusivity that makes it a very Venetian garden.

THIS PAGE – *In the centre of a lawn, exceptional for Venice both in size and condition, is an old Pagoda tree,* Sophora japonica, *planted in the 1920's, before much of the garden was taken for housing.*

THIS PAGE – *Trachelospermum and roses in full flower smother the walls of the palazzo, flanking iron gates and a barred window leading from the garden to an interior courtyard.*

Palazzo Gradenigo has two gardens. One is permanent, belonging to the owner Toto Bergamo Rossi, the other temporary in so much that it has been made by one of the occupants in the apartments that make up the palazzo, Anthony Santospirito. Anthony (known to all as Kaj) and his wife Skye and their two sons split their time between London and Venice, but it is much more than a holiday home. It is a base and the garden is an integral part of that. Skye was brought up in Venice to British parents and they are hefted there. Kaj, Australian of Italian descent, loves plants and is extremely knowledgeable about them but his passion is for nurturing them. 'A garden is a chance to grow things healthily,' he says, by which he means that a garden is where he strives to give each plant the conditions and care that allow it to be most fully its best natural self – rather than the man-made conception of what a plant should be, that dominated so much of twentieth-century horticulture.

As a result his garden is an eclectic joy. You approach from their first floor apartment from a wisteria-clad terrace down a spiral staircase inextricably enveloped in a fig as though climbing down from a figgy tree house. The first impression is quite unlike any other Venetian garden I have seen. It is a flower-studded wilderness where even a cursory second glance reveals an unusually wide range of plants, each looking spectacularly healthy and performing at the top of its floral bent.

Although small it is crammed with plants, all in a loose and informal swathe, and Kaj seems to have a deep personal bond with each and every one of them. There is a lawn but, predictably, it is strikingly un-Venetian. In May the unmown grass was dotted with tulips, fritillaries both meleagris and michailovskyi, camassias, poppies and alliums. Despite having no rain the previous winter for six months these moisture-loving flowers – fritillaries, camassias – have been nourished by a leaking irrigation system from Toto's garden the other side of the hedge that divides them.

Bearded irises were in full voluptuous bloom in the borders; pale blues, caramel brown, bright yellow, mixed white and mauve and particularly beautiful rich burgundy ones that were given from the intensely private Volpi garden on the Giudecca. Rather than stand alone as floral trophies as bearded irises so often are, these stood out from a backdrop of feathery fennel, the foliage of unopened lilies – *Henryi*, Madonna, *regale* and *speciosum* every one a character and individual to Kaj as he showed me round. A shrubby backdrop of elder and ligustrum creates an informal, unclipped hedge. Pots stood in the grass and against the wall, with gingers, cardamon, nasturtiums and cobea – all of which survive the Venetian winter to thrive in its spring and summer. Aquilegias, hostas, violets and hepatica weave loosely together. In fact, looseness is the main feature of the garden, plants melding and jostling with each other in an entirely informal parade – yet one that is clearly monitored and tended with precision by Kaj's guiding hand. He tells the story of each plant as we go round the garden, both personal and botanical, clearly endlessly fascinated and delighted by them.

THIS PAGE – *The garden of Kaj Santospirito is only separated from Toto Bergamo Rossi's garden by a hedge but is completely different in style and content, having a very carefully cultured informality.*

OPPOSITE – *A large wisteria clambers up the spiral staircase leading to the apartment in the palazzo.*

THIS PAGE – *The planting of these lilies, iris, nasturtiums and fronds of fennel is a brilliant display of informal, eclectic but very carefully chosen combinations of colour, texture and form where plants weave and meld together.*

NEXT PAGE – *Field poppies grow in a corner of the lawn that is under planted with a wide range of bulbs and annual wild flowers.*

Most of this is grown from seed or cuttings and slips of plants given by friends. His gardener's fingers are green and it seems that plants want to do well for him – although that story is always an inversion of the real truth, which is that the successful gardener is one that does well by their plants rather than a lucky gift. He has compost bins under the shade of a large yew, building the fertility of the sandy, salty soil. The climate and soil provide horticultural quirks such as the only sweet pea that seems to survive is Cupani, with the bigger Spencer varieties failing miserably and only single dahlias prosper. But the one bonus of the salt, he tells me, is the almost complete absence of slugs or snails and the thin soil means mint, such an invasive thug in my own garden, can grow freely without ever outgrowing its space or welcome. Hostas seem completely happy despite the thin soil and lack of rainfall – although the high water table must play its role in that and Venetian winters are traditionally wet and cold and the summers hot and dry, although climate change, as everywhere, may be changing that pattern completely.

We have lunch outside on a table set in the long grass, a setting as informal as an English country vicarage and as exotic as a palazzo in the middle of Venice. It is a perfect combination.

OPPOSITE – *Regal lilies growing in pots raised on plinths standing in the grass. Kaj grows a wide range of plants in pots that can then be moved around the garden to display them in flower.*

THIS PAGE – *Beautiful but also much-used tools. Unlike most Venetian gardeners, Kaj does all his own propagating and maintenance.*

INDEX

Note: page numbers in **bold** *refer to information contained in captions.*

BBC Books, an imprint of Ebury Publishing,
20 Vauxhall Bridge Road,
London SW1V 2SA

BBC Books is part of the Penguin Random House group
of companies whose addresses can be found at global.
penguinrandomhouse.com

Text copyright © Monty Don 2022

Photography copyright © Derry Moore 2022

Monty Don and Derry Moore have asserted their right to be
identified as the authors of this Work in accordance with the
Copyright, Designs and Patents Act 1988

First published by BBC Books in 2022

www.penguin.co.uk

A CIP catalogue record for this book is available from the British
Library

ISBN 9781785947421

Publishing Director: Albert DePetrillo
Project Editor: Charlotte Macdonald
Design: Lucie Stericker/studio 7:15
Production: Antony Heller

Printed and bound in Italy by Graphicom S.p.A.

Penguin Random House is committed to a sustainable future for our
business, our readers and our planet. This book is made from Forest
Stewardship Council® certified paper.

ACKNOWLEDGEMENTS

MONTY DON

My first thanks must be to all the owners and custodians of
the gardens in Venice that opened their doors to us with such
hospitality and generosity.

Special thanks must go to Mariagrazia Dammicco for her expert
advice, experience and introductions, but the whole team in
Venice that transported, advised and guided us from garden to
garden were superb.

Garrett Moore was an invaluable researcher and minder, as well
as being a wonderful companion.

At every stage, from conception to completion, Alexandra
Henderson was the guiding spirit and collaborator and, as ever,
I owe her a huge debt of gratitude.

At Ebury, Albert DePetrillo showed great calm and forbearance
as the best laid plans and deadlines went astray.

But the greatest thanks are to my wife Sarah, because without her,
none of this would be.

DERRY MOORE

To make a book of this nature requires enormous help from a
variety of people. Without this help the book would not have been
possible. In addition to the people Monty has mentioned, as the
photographer there are a number of others, who I would like to
thank. These include:

Bianca Arrivabene and her assistants Sue Ellen Pavin and
Mascia Pavon.

My old friend Verde Visconti, who re-introduced me to Contessa
Cristiana Brandolini, thereby enabling me to photograph the
wonderful garden at Palazzo Brandolini.

Special thanks to Kaj Santospirito and Skye McAlpine who not
only allowed us to photograph their wonderful garden, but also
generously had my wife Alexandra and me to stay.

The logistics of working in Venice are particularly complicated
and these aspects were greatly helped by Laura Venturini, my son
Garrett Moore, as well as Pieter Jurriaanse, who patiently and
imaginatively took me through many canals in his boat.

My assistant in London Raffaella Matrone, whose help,
particularly where her Italian and knowledge of Venice were
concerned, was invaluable, as well as her general efficiency.

To Lucie Stericker who has done the layout of this book, a task
requiring considerable patience and tolerance, in view of the
frequent changes that were required.

To Antony Heller at Ebury Press for his support.

As always, my thanks to Brent Wallace whose editing and
correcting skills were of immense help.